Contents at a Glance

Wireless Networking

with Microsoft® Windows *Vista*™

Michael Miller

800 East 96th Street,
Indianapolis, Indiana 46240

Wireless Networking with Microsoft® Windows Vista™

ISBN-13: 978-0-7897-3701-9
ISBN-10: 0-7897-3701-9

Library of Congress Cataloging-in-Publication Data

Miller, Michael, 1958-
  Wireless networking with Microsoft Windows Vista / Michael Miller.
    p. cm.
  ISBN 0-7897-3701-9
  1. Wireless communication systems. 2. Computer networks. 3. Microsoft Windows (Computer file) I. Title.
  TK5103.2.M554 2007
  004.6—dc22

                                        2007021598

Printed in the United States of America

First Printing: July 2007

Trademarks

All terms mentioned in this book that are known to be trademarks or service marks have been appropriately capitalized. Que Publishing cannot attest to the accuracy of this information. Use of a term in this book should not be regarded as affecting the validity of any trademark or service mark.

Warning and Disclaimer

Every effort has been made to make this book as complete and as accurate as possible, but no warranty or fitness is implied. The information provided is on an "as is" basis. The author and the publisher shall have neither liability nor responsibility to any person or entity with respect to any loss or damages arising from the information contained in this book..

Bulk Sales

Que Publishing offers excellent discounts on this book when ordered in quantity for bulk purchases or special sales. For more information, please contact

U.S. Corporate and Government Sales
1-800-382-3419
corpsales@pearsontechgroup.com

For sales outside the U.S., please contact

International Sales
international@pearsoned.com

Publisher
Paul Boger

Associate Publisher
Greg Wiegand

Acquisitions Editor
Rick Kughen

Development Editor
Rick Kughen

Managing Editor
Gina Kanouse

Project Editor
George Nedeff

Copy Editor
Geneil Breeze

Senior Indexer
Cheryl Lenser

Proofreader
Carla Lewis

Technical Editor
Karen Weinstein

Publishing Coordinator
Cindy Teeters

Book Designer
Anne Jones

Compositor
Nonie Ratcliff

This Book Is Safari Enabled

The Safari® Enabled icon on the cover of your favorite technology book means the book is available through Safari Bookshelf. When you buy this book, you get free access to the online edition for 45 days.

Safari Bookshelf is an electronic reference library that lets you easily search thousands of technical books, find code samples, download chapters, and access technical information whenever and wherever you need it.

To gain 45-day Safari Enabled access to this book:

- Go to http://www.quepublishing.com/safarienabled
- Complete the brief registration form
- Enter the coupon code 4NKF-6ULJ-VLV4-V9JV-TGZ3

If you have difficulty registering on Safari Bookshelf or accessing the online edition, please email customer-service@safaribooksonline.com.

Table of Contents

About the Author

Michael Miller has written more than 75 nonfiction how-to books in the past two decades, including Que's *Googlepedia: The Ultimate Google Resource*, *iPodpedia: The Ultimate iPod and iTunes Resource*, *Absolute Beginner's Guide to Computer Basics*, *Absolute Beginner's Guide to eBay*, and *How Microsoft Windows Vista Works*. He also writes about digital lifestyle topics for a number of websites.

Mr. Miller has established a reputation for clearly explaining technical topics to nontechnical readers, and for offering useful real-world advice about complicated topics. More information can be found at the author's website, located at www.molehillgroup.com.

Dedication

To Sherry, you'll always be part of my network.

Acknowledgments

Thanks to the usual suspects at Que Publishing, including but not limited to Greg Wiegand, Rick Kughen, George Nedeff, Geneil Breeze, and technical editor Karen Weinstein.

We Want to Hear from You!

As the reader of this book, *you* are our most important critic and commentator. We value your opinion and want to know what we're doing right, what we could do better, what areas you'd like to see us publish in, and any other words of wisdom you're willing to pass our way.

As an associate publisher for Que Publishing, I welcome your comments. You can email or write me directly to let me know what you did or didn't like about this book—as well as what we can do to make our books better.

Please note that I cannot help you with technical problems related to the topic of this book. We do have a User Services group, however, where I will forward specific technical questions related to the book.

When you write, please be sure to include this book's title and author as well as your name, email address, and phone number. I will carefully review your comments and share them with the author and editors who worked on the book.

Email: feedback@quepublishing.com

Mail: Greg Wiegand
          Associate Publisher
          Que Publishing
          800 East 96th Street
          Indianapolis, IN 46240 USA

Reader Services

Visit our website and register this book at www.quepublishing.com/register for convenient access to any updates, downloads, or errata that might be available for this book.

Introduction

It's funny how things change.

Just a few short years ago, setting up a computer network was the province of specially trained, highly technical network administrators. You almost needed a degree in network administration to choose the proper equipment, run the appropriate wiring, and configure all the technical settings. It was not for the technically casual user, or for the faint of heart.

And that equipment? Back in the day, it was expensive—very expensive. Putting together a home or small business network might set you back a thousand bucks or so, all things considered. Costly, to say the least.

Physically setting up the network was also a chore. Everything was wired, so you had to run and connect what seemed like miles of Ethernet cable. Depending on where your computers were located, you might have to run that cable through walls and ceilings, through attics and basements, around corners and under carpets. It was a real pain in the posterior, on the best of days.

After you had everything purchased, positioned, and connected, you then had to deal with the technical configuration. If your computers were running Windows 95 or some similarly ancient operating system, this process was completely unintuitive. (Hence the need for formal network training.) You had to deal with all manner of indecipherable acronyms, addresses, and settings; nothing was logical, nothing was readily apparent, nothing was easy.

Fortunately for you, things are much different now. Networking equipment has come down in price, so that thousand-dollar network will only cost you a few hundred dollars today. The equipment is a lot easier to configure and use, and things are completely wireless—so there are no more messy cables to run. Even better, newer versions of Windows have internalized much of the network setup and configuration, so that setting up your computer for network use is as easy as clicking a few buttons.

If you're running Windows Vista on your network computers, things are even easier. Some of the best behind-the-scenes improvements in the new Vista operating system involve networking. With Vista, networking is both easier to set up (often automatically, with little or no interaction on your part) and more stable. With Vista, networking just works.

That doesn't mean, however, that you don't have questions or need any assistance. You still need to know what kind of network to create, what equipment you need to buy, how to connect all that equipment, and then how to configure everything to work the way you want it. And then, of course, there's the issue of what to do when things don't work like they're supposed to.

That's where this book comes in. *Wireless Networking with Windows Vista* is your complete guide to connecting Windows Vista PCs in a home or small business network. Whether you're creating a new network from scratch, upgrading your current network, connecting a new PC to an existing network, or connecting a notebook PC to a public wireless hot spot, this book will help you do what you need to do.

How This Book Is Organized

Wireless Networking with Windows Vista contains a lot of information about setting up and using wireless networks. To make finding the right information easier, this book is organized into five main parts, each focused on a particular aspect of the networking process:

- **Part I, "Planning Your Wireless Network,"** provides an introduction to wireless networking, describes the different types of Wi-Fi networks available, helps you design your new network, and provides advice for purchasing the appropriate networking equipment.

- **Part II, "Setting Up Your Wireless Network,"** is where you get your hands dirty, so to speak. Here you'll find step-by-step instructions for connecting all your network computers and equipment, configuring all the devices on your network, setting up and sharing a wireless Internet connection, and adding wireless security to your network.

- **Part III, "Using Your Wireless Network,"** shows you how to use your network for various day-to-day tasks. You'll learn how to set up your network for multiple users, share files and folders, share music and other media, share printers and other peripherals, and connect video game systems to your wireless network.

- **Part IV, "Using Other Networks,"** takes wireless networking outside the home. Read this section to learn how to connect your Windows Vista notebook to a Wi-Fi hot spot, or to a corporate network at work.

- **Part V, "Upgrading and Maintaining Your Wireless Network,"** is the section to read if you want to connect additional devices to your network, or if you're experiencing any sort of network-related problems. (The troubleshooting advice in the final chapter may be worth the entire price of the book!)

Finally, we end the book with a glossary of networking terms, which is useful if you don't know your 802.11g from your IP addresses. All those confusing terms are explained here.

Conventions Used in This Book

I hope that this book is easy enough to figure out on its own, without requiring its own instruction manual. As you read through the pages, however, it helps to know precisely how I've presented specific types of information.

Menu Commands

Windows Vista presents an intuitive point-and-click interface. To indicate navigation through Windows and various software programs, I use the following notation:

> Main menu, Submenu, Submenu.

All you have to do is follow the instructions in order, using your mouse to click through the various menus and submenus. For example, if I tell you to open the Start menu and select All Programs, Accessories, System Tools, you know to click the Start button and select the various menus and submenus in order. It's pretty easy.

Web Pages and Manufacturer Information

Obviously, there are lots of web page addresses in the book, like this one: www.mole-hillgroup.com. When you see one of these addresses (also known as a *URL*), you can go to that web page by entering the URL into the address box in your web browser. I've made every effort to ensure the accuracy of the web addresses presented here, but given the ever-changing nature of the Web, don't be surprised if you run across an address or two that's changed. I apologize in advance.

Many of the web pages listed in this book are those of networking equipment manufacturers. In fact, you'll find a lot of network-related equipment discussed in this book. These listings are for your information only; just because I describe a particular item doesn't mean I personally endorse it. (In many instances, comparable equipment from different manufacturers is equally deserving.) Know that the prices mentioned in this book are current as of April 2007 and are retail prices suggested by the manufacturer; actual street prices might be and probably are lower, depending on where and when you shop.

Special Elements

As you read through this book you'll note several special elements, presented in what we in the publishing business call "margin notes." Different types of margin notes are used for different types of information, as you see here.

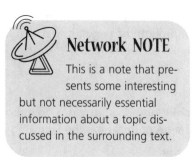

Network NOTE
This is a note that presents some interesting but not necessarily essential information about a topic discussed in the surrounding text.

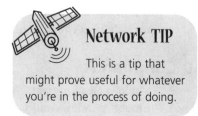

Network TIP
This is a tip that might prove useful for whatever you're in the process of doing.

Network CAUTION
This is a caution that something you might accidentally do might have undesirable results—so take care!

There's More on the Web

Now that you know how to use this book, it's time to get to the heart of the matter. But when you're ready to take a break from setting up your new wireless network, you may also want to check out my personal website, located at www.molehill-group.com. Here you'll find more information about all the other books I've written and am in the process of writing. I'll also post any updates or corrections to this book, in the inevitable event that an error or two creeps into this text. (Hey, nobody's perfect!)

In addition, know that I love to hear from readers of my books. If you want to contact me, feel free to email me at networking@molehillgroup.com. I can't promise that I'll answer every message, but I do promise that I'll read each one!

But enough with the preliminaries. Turn the page and start networking!

Part I

Planning Your Wireless Network

In this chapter

Why You Need a Wireless Network

You have a computer. Maybe more than one. You have a printer, maybe more than one, connected to that computer. You might even have a laptop computer for home or business use. And you have a connection to the Internet.

If this describes your house or office, you're a prime candidate for a wireless computer network. Why is that? Read on and learn.

What Is a Network?

A computer network is, put simply, two or more computers or similar devices connected together. When the computers are connected, they can send electronic signals back and forth. This lets them communicate with each other (via email or instant messaging) and share things. The computers on a network can share files—that is, one computer can access the files stored on another computer. They can share printers, by sending their print requests over the network to the PC that is physically connected to the printer. They can share a single Internet connection. They can even share software applications. (Think multiple-player games here.)

Obviously, there are many ways to connect computers together in a network and many different types of equipment you can use; you can also create fancier networks with more than two computers, peripherals, Internet connection sharing, and the like. But the fact remains, to create a network you have to connect at least two things together.

We'll get into the specifics of network types and equipment elsewhere in this book. For now, know that you can connect the computers and devices in your network using cables or via some type of wireless connection. Whether your network is wired or wireless, everything ultimately connects to a network router, which functions as the hub for all network operations and communications. Each computer connects to the router and sends data and other signals through the router to other computers on the network.

This simple description of a simple network is valid for most small networks that connect computers in a single location—home networks, small office networks, and the like. These simple networks are called *local area networks*, or *LANs*. Larger networks that encompass computers in multiple locations (such as in several different offices of a corporation) are called *wide area networks*, or *WANs*. A WAN is considerably more complex to set up and manage than is a LAN; WANs typically require network administrators to keep everything working on a day-to-day basis.

Most LANs, on the other hand, don't require a lot of technical expertise, either to set up or to keep running. A basic home network, for example, can be set up in less than an hour by anyone with a nominal level of computer experience. Small office networks are seldom more complex.

In other words, it's possible for you to set up your own computer network, with a minimal investment in time and money. But why would you want to do so?

Network NOTE

For purposes of this book, I assume that you are setting up a network in your home or small office and, thus, I only cover LANs—not WANs.

Multiple-Computer Networks: Sharing Files and More

The most common reason to set up a computer network is that you have more than one computer in your home or office, and you want to share files between those computers. A local area network is, after all, a means to connect multiple computers. If you have two (or three or four) computers in your environment, it makes sense to connect them together in a small computer network.

To share files without a network, you have to copy those files from your first computer to some sort of physical media, such as a CD-ROM or USB memory drive, walk that CD or USB drive to a second computer, and then copy the files from that drive to the second PC. As you can see in Figure 1.1, it's a time-consuming process, and maybe not even be possible if your files are larger than the storage medium can hold.

FIGURE 1.1

Copying files the old-school way—physically moving files from one computer to another.

When you connect your computers to a network, file sharing gets a lot easier. All you have to do is use Windows to copy the files from one computer to another, which is similar to copying files from one folder to another on the same computer. As you can see in Figure 1.2, there's nothing physical to handle, no size constraints, and the whole process is a lot less time consuming; the copying is almost instantaneous.

Network NOTE
The process of physically carrying files and media from one computer to another is often called the *sneaker net*, in deference to the footwear sometimes used by the human file transporters.

FIGURE 1.2

Copying files over a computer network—nothing physical to handle.

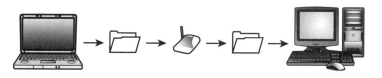

Beyond the increased convenience, there's also the ability to open files stored on one computer from a second computer, no copying needed. That's right, one computer can store the file while another computer opens it; a single file thus can be shared between multiple users on multiple computers. As you can see in Figure 1.3, this saves on disk space, as you don't have to duplicate that file on each computer.

FIGURE 1.3
Sharing a file over a network.

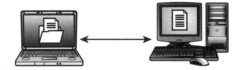

And then there's another benefit to copying and sharing files between computers—the ability to back up your data files from one computer to another. You can use one computer (or an external hard drive connected to that computer) to store the backup data from a second computer, and vice versa. It's much more convenient than backing up your data to blank CDs or tapes.

Network NOTE

Learn more about network file sharing in Chapter 10, "Sharing Files and Folders."

Media-Sharing Networks: Music and Movies in Your Office and Your Living Room

The concept of network-based file sharing becomes even more important in the digital media age. It's not just Word and Excel files you can share; you can also share music, movies, photographs, and more.

Let's say you have your main computer in your office, on which is stored hundreds (if not thousands) of digital music files that you've ripped from CD or downloaded from the Internet. If you want to listen to those tracks in your living room, over your home audio system, how do you do it?

The answer is to invest in a second computer, place it in your living room, and connect your two computers over a home network. The living room computer doesn't need a big hard disk, but it does need to connect to your home audio system. (Just run an audio cable from your PC's audio out jack to your audio system's audio in jacks.) Now, thanks to the magic of network-based file sharing, you can

Network TIP

If your media library is big enough, you might even want to invest in a big network drive to house all the media files. This is a shared hard disk drive that connects to your network and can be accessed by all your network PCs.

use the PC in your living room to access and play the music files stored on the PC in your office. You don't have to copy the files from one PC to another, or store them twice; as you can see in Figure 1.4, the living room PC simply uses the network to play the files stored on the other computer.

FIGURE 1.4

Using two network PCs to play music in your living room.

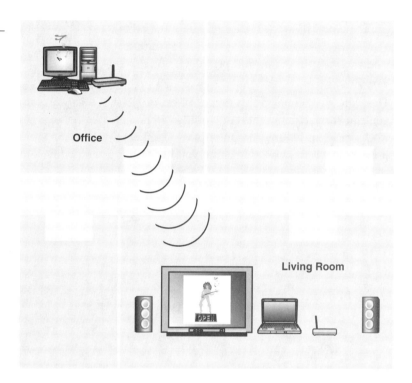

Office

Living Room

The same concept applies to other types of digital media—movies and other videos, digital photographs, you name it. Store the movies or photos on any PC with a big hard drive, and view them on a smaller PC located in your living room (or any other room in your house, for that matter).

Network NOTE

Learn more about network media sharing in Chapter 11, "Sharing Music, Movies, and Other Digital Media."

Printer-Sharing Networks: Getting More Out of a Single Piece of Equipment

Just as a network lets you share files between multiple computers, it can also let you share computer peripherals between those same PCs. That is, you can connect a single peripheral, such as a printer or scanner, to your network and then access that peripheral from any network PC.

Let's take the most common example of this practice, the network printer. Without a network, you would have to purchase separate printers for each individual PC in your home or office. With a network, however, you only need to purchase a single printer. As you can see in Figure 1.5, connect that printer to any network PC, and then all the other PCs on the network can access and print to that printer. One printer for multiple PCs; it's a real cost saver.

There are variations on this theme, of course. First, you can connect more than one printer to the network, and thus let any computer print to either printer. This is a good approach if you have a black-and-white letter printer and a color photo printer, for example.

Network NOTE

Don't be frightened by the phrase *network printer*. A network printer is any printer, large or small, that is connected to and shared by a network. (In other words, you don't have to buy a special printer to connect to your network; any printer will do the job.)

FIGURE 1.5

Sharing a single printer between multiple network PCs.

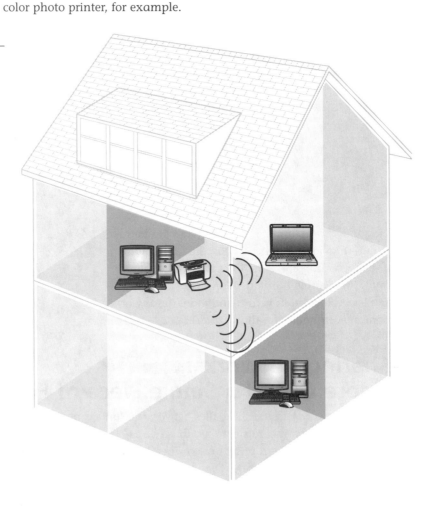

Second, you don't have to connect the network printer to a network PC. Instead, you can use a small device called a *print server*, which connects directly to your network router. Connect your printer to the print server, and thus to your router, and you can place that printer anywhere in your home office; it doesn't have to sit right next to one of your computers.

Network NOTE

Learn more about printer sharing in Chapter 12, "Sharing Printers and Other Peripherals."

Finally, you're not limited to sharing printers over a network. You can share all sorts of other peripherals, including scanners, external hard disks, even Internet modems—which we'll discuss next.

Internet-Sharing Networks: Going Online from Anywhere in Your House

Today, one of the biggest driving forces for home networking is Internet connection sharing. That is, you have a single Internet connection coming into your house, and you want every computer in your home to access that connection. Sharing an Internet connection requires setting up some sort of home network—even if you never intend to share files or peripherals.

Network NOTE

A *wireless access point* is a standalone Wi-Fi transmitter/receiver without net-work routing capabilities.

As you can see in Figure 1.6, sharing an Internet connection involves connecting your broadband modem to a network router or wireless access point, and then connecting all your computers to that router, as well. The modem typically connects to the router via a short cable, while the computers more often than not connect wirelessly.

Network NOTE

Learn more about Internet connection sharing in Chapter 7, "Setting Up—And Sharing—A Wireless Internet Connection."

Connected as such, each computer on the network can independently access the Internet. One computer can be checking email while another surfs the Web and a third is playing games and instant messaging. The single Internet connection becomes a big pipe that transmits data to and from each of the connected computers—thanks to networking technology.

FIGURE 1.6

Sharing an
Internet connec-
tion over a
network.

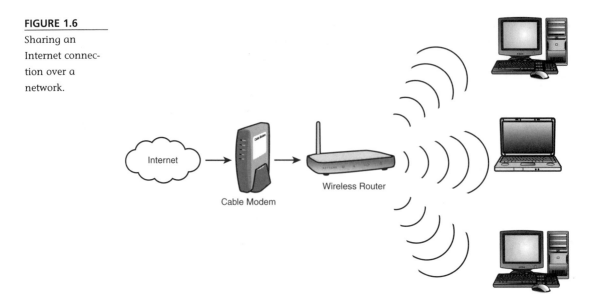

Laptop-Based Networks: Cutting the Cable

Remember how I previously defined a network as connecting two or more computers or similar devices? That number (two) isn't hard and fast; you can create a network with just a single computer.

The best example of this involves a portable PC and an Internet connection.
Normally, you'd have to connect this single PC via a short cable to your broadband
Internet modem. This type of setup, however, significantly reduces the mobility of
the PC; you're tied to the modem if you want to connect to the Internet.

To regain this lost mobility, you create a simple wireless network, such as the one
shown in Figure 1.7. In this simple network, the Internet connection goes into the
wireless network router; the notebook PC then connects to the router wirelessly, from
anywhere in the house, to access the Internet. Place the modem and router in your
office, and you can sit in your living room or bedroom and surf the Web. You're not
using the file- or peripheral-sharing capabilities of the network, but you don't need
to; all you want to do is connect to the Internet from wherever you have your
laptop today.

FIGURE 1.7

Sharing an
Internet con-
nection over a
network.

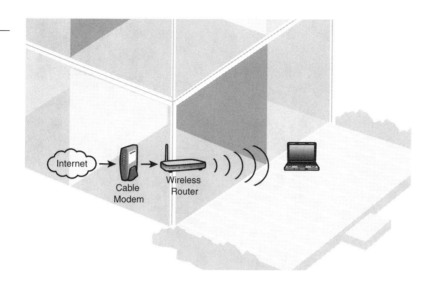

Game-Playing Networks: Connecting Your Video Game Console to the Internet

Finally, there may be a noncomputer reason to establish a computer network. If you
have a new-generation video game system—Nintendo Wii, Sony PlayStation 3, or
Microsoft Xbox 360—you know that your game console has Internet-related functionality. Depending on the console, you may be able to connect to the Internet to
download new games, play games with other users, or even access news and email.

To do this, of course, you need to connect your
game console to the Internet. And what do you do
if your Internet connection is in your office and
your game console is in your living room or
basement?

The answer is to set up a wireless network, such as
the one shown in Figure 1.8. Like the notebook-
based network described previously, you connect
your broadband modem to a wireless network
router, and then connect a wireless adapter to your
game console. The game console connects to your wireless network and thus gains
access to the Internet—no cables to run, nothing complicated to configure.

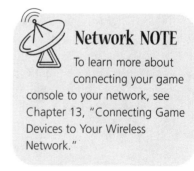

Network NOTE

To learn more about
connecting your game
console to your network, see
Chapter 13, "Connecting Game
Devices to Your Wireless
Network."

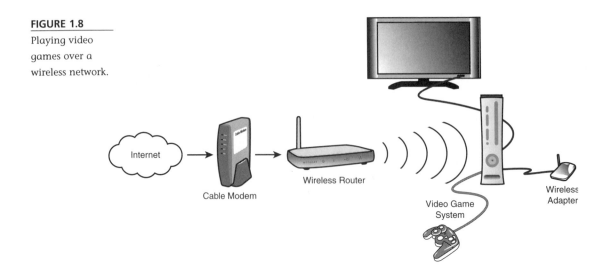

What Type of Network Do You Need?

It's likely that at least one of these scenarios is reason enough for you to set up a network in your home or small office. In fact, after you have your network set up and configured, you can use it for any or all of these functions. Set up a simple network for use with a video game, and you can later connect a laptop computer to share that same Internet connection. Set up a network to share a printer between two computers, and you can later add a third computer in your living room to share music and movie files. You get the idea.

However you choose to use your network, you must choose between building a wired or a wireless network. Most wired networks today use Ethernet technology to transfer data at up to 1 gigabit per second (Gbps), which is pretty fast. Although the speed is nice, the chief drawback to a wired network is the wire. Not only do you have to deal with running long stretches of Ethernet cable, you also have to pay for all that cable. You may also have difficulty running cable through doorways, up and down stairs, and so on.

The alternative to a wired network is a wireless network. The advantage of wireless, of course, is that you don't have to run any cables. This is a big plus if you have a large house with computers on either end or on different floors. And it's a necessity if you want to connect a notebook PC and not be tethered to the network router.

Most wireless networks today use the 802.11g Wi-Fi standard, which transfers data at 54 megabits per second (Mbps). Although this is considerably slower than Gigabit Ethernet (1Gbps = 1,000Mbps), it's fast enough for most home networking needs. (For example, most Internet connections are only in the 1-2Mbps neighborhood, which makes even a 54Mbps network speed overkill.) Unless you transfer a lot of really large files from one computer to another or play real-time multiplayer online PC games, a wireless network will be more than fast enough for your needs.

Of course, your network doesn't have to be just wired or wireless—it can be a hybrid of the two. In fact, most home networks have some computers connected wirelessly, and others connected via Ethernet. It's easy enough to do, and plays on the strengths of both types of networks.

Next: How Wireless Networks Work

Setting up a wireless network is also fairly easy, especially because you don't have to deal with a lot of Ethernet cabling. But just how does a wireless network do what it needs to do? That's what you'll find out in Chapter 2, "How Wireless Networks Work"; turn the page to learn more.

In this chapter

2

How Wireless Networks Work

Connecting one computer to another seems easy enough, but in reality this process utilizes some very advanced technology. The wireless part of a wireless network uses radio signals at a specific frequency, which means you essentially build a mini-radio station in your home or office. The business of transmitting data signals between PCs involves a complex set of networking protocols, so that each computer knows what's coming and going—and in what fashion. All this technical complexity happens behind the scenes, of course, but it does have to happen.

Networking Basics

One of the challenges of creating a computer network is sending the data from one computer to another. Naturally, the networking hardware you install handles the physical part of this transaction, but the hardware has to work in tandem with a predescribed set of networking transfer protocols—a set of rules that determine how data is transmitted across the network.

Understanding TCP/IP

There are several different network protocols that your network could use, but the one most used in home and small business networks is *TCP/IP (Transmission Control Protocol/Internet Protocol)*. This particular protocol is used in all Windows-based computer networks.

Network NOTE

TCP/IP is also the transport protocol for the Internet—which is itself a super-network of networks.

The IP part of the protocol provides the standard set of rules and specifications that enable the routing of data packets from one network to another. The TCP part of the protocol supports process-to-process communication between two computers; it takes network information and translates it into a form that your network can understand. In other words, IP sets the rules, and TCP does the interpreting of those rules.

As illustrated in Figure 2.1, here's how it works in practice:

1. Let's say you want to copy a file from the PC in your home office to the PC located in your basement. When you click the Copy button, TCP establishes a connection between the two computers; then IP lays down the rules of communication and connects the ports of the two computers.

2. Because TCP has prepared the data for transmittal, IP then takes the file, breaks it into smaller pieces (called *packets*), and puts a header on each packet to make sure it gets to where it's going. The TCP packet is also labeled with the kind of data it's carrying and how large the packet is.

3. Next, IP converts the packet into a standard format and sends it on its way from the first computer to the second.

4. After the packet is received by the second PC, TCP translates the packet into its original format and combines the multiple packets back into a single file.

FIGURE 2.1
How TCP/IP
transmits data
from one PC to
another.

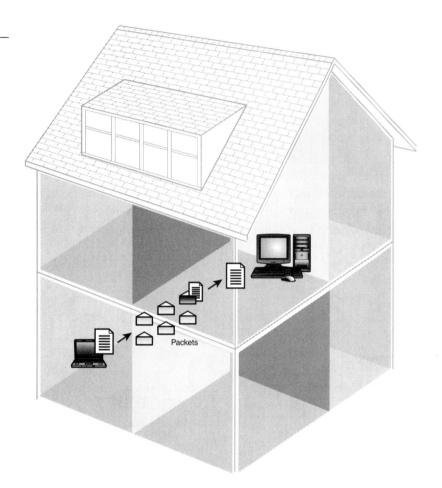

Understanding Network Addresses

For TCP/IP to work, each of your computers needs to be properly configured with the proper information. In particular, you need to assign each computer a local IP address, which is how the computer is known by the network.

Assuming you've spent time on the Internet, you've already seen some IP addresses. An IP address is a numeric identifier that looks like this:

192.106.126.193

On the Internet, each website has its own IP address, which is tied to an easier-to-remember web address (called a *URL*), in the form of www.*url*.com. In the case of computer networks, an IP address is the software address of an individual PC; every computer on your network has its own individual IP address.

You may also need to assign a *subnet mask*, which identifies which part of the network the computer belongs to. In essence, a subnet mask is a number that is overlaid onto the computer's IP address. In the case of most smaller networks, the subnet is the same as the IP address; on larger networks, different subnets may exist. Assuming that you are setting up a small private wireless network for use at home or in a small business, however, you probably won't need to worry about subnet masks.

These addresses are necessary for the network router to know which data goes to which computer. As you can see in Figure 2.2, TCP/IP broadcasts data to the router, with a particular IP address identified as the recipient of that data. The router reads the IP address, and then routes the data to the computer with that address.

FIGURE 2.2
How TCP/IP transmits data from one PC to another.

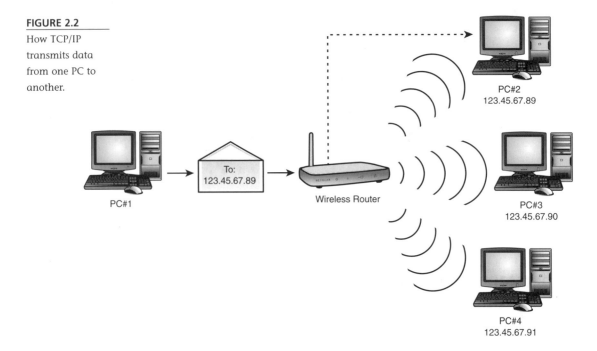

All this sounds rather daunting, and on older operating systems it was; you had to configure all these addresses manually. But in Windows Vista, this configuration is done automatically, which makes it easy enough for even technical novices to set up.

Comparing Wired and Wireless Networks

Networking protocols define how data is transmitted from one computer to another; the actual transmission of that data can be done via Ethernet cables or wireless signals.

Understanding Ethernet Networks

Ethernet is a cabling protocol developed by Xerox, DEC, and Intel for transmitting data across local area networks. As shown in Figure 2.3, an Ethernet network requires installing network interface cards (NICs) in each computer on the network, and then using Ethernet cables to connect each computer/NIC to a central network router. The router does as its name implies—it routes data packets from one network computer to another.

FIGURE 2.3

A typical Ethernet network.

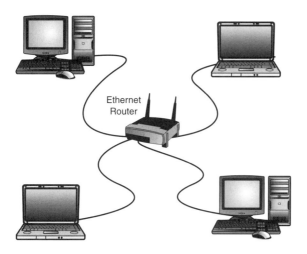

Ethernet networks come in three speeds: So-called Gigabit Ethernet transfers data at 1Gbps; Fast Ethernet operates at a tenth that speed, or 100Mbps; and older 10Base-T Ethernet is a tenth of that, at 10Mbps. Exempting the older 10Mbps Ethernet standard, today's Ethernet networks are considerably faster than today's wireless networks. (Although there is a faster wireless standard in the works—which we'll discuss in a moment.)

Understanding Wireless Networks

A wireless network does away with the network cards and Ethernet cables, instead using radio frequency (RF) signals to connect one computer to another. Each computer on the network must have a wireless adapter installed; this adapter is essentially a miniature transmitter/receiver for the RF signals. Data is then transmitted from each computer's wireless adapter to a wireless router (sometimes called a *base station* or *residential gateway device*), as shown in Figure 2.4. The wireless router, like the wireless adapters, functions as both a transmitter and receiver for the wireless signals.

When data is transmitted over a wireless network, a sophisticated set of technologies is put into play. The wireless router serves as the hub of this wireless section, not only routing the network data but also broadcasting the name of the network (called a *Service Set Identifier*, or *SSID*) over a beacon signal. This beacon is broadcast every 100 milliseconds and enables nearby wireless adapters to recognize and communicate with the wireless network.

When connected to the wireless router, the individual wireless adapter transmits the selected data from its connected computer in the customary data packets, via RF signals. Most wireless networks transmit data in the 2.4GHz frequency band, which is a "free" and unregulated range of signals.

 Network NOTE

A wireless adapter can be a small external device that connects to a PC via USB, an expansion card that installs inside your system unit, or a PC card that inserts into a portable PC's card slot. Additionally, most newer notebook PCs come with a built-in wireless adapter, no external cards or devices necessary. Some newer desktop PCs are shipping with a wireless adapter built-in, too, making it a snap to add a new PC to your wireless network.

FIGURE 2.4

A typical wireless network.

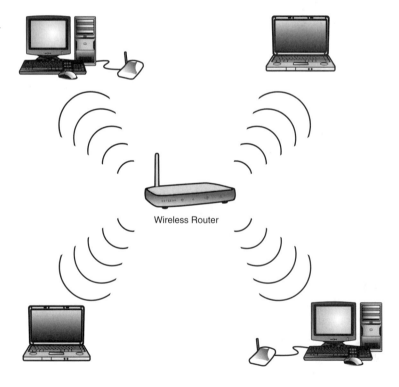

Wireless Router

The main advantage of a wireless network, of course, is that you don't have to run any cables, or install network cards in all your PCs. This is a big plus if you have a large house with computers on either end, or on different floors.

Alphabet Soup: Different Types of Wi-Fi

Network CAUTION

The 2.4GHz RF band is used by many different types of electronic devices, including cordless phones, microwave ovens, baby monitors, and the like. These devices can create interference with a wireless network, typically in the form of data or signal loss.

Today's wireless networks use a type of RF transmission called *Wi-Fi* (short for *wireless fidelity*), which is the consumer-friendly name for the IEEE 802.11 wireless networking standard. This standard was developed by an industry group called the Wi-Fi Alliance.

But here's the thing. There isn't a single Wi-Fi protocol. Instead, there are multiple 802.11 protocols, each designated by a single-letter suffix. Different versions of Wi-Fi offer different levels of performance; which of these Wi-Fi standards you choose for your wireless network depends on your needs—and the equipment currently available for purchase.

Network NOTE

Learn more about the Wi-Fi standard at the Wi-Fi Alliance website (www.wi-fi.org).

Table 2.1 summarizes the specifications of the most popular 802.11 protocols for consumer use. More details on each version follow.

Table 2.1 Wi-Fi Protocols

Wi-Fi Protocol	Release Date	Frequency Range	Data Transfer Rate (Max)	Transmission Range (Indoor)
802.11a	1999	5.0GHz	54Mbps	80 feet
802.11b	1999	2.4GHz	11Mbps	115 feet
802.11g	2003	2.4GHz	54Mbps	100 feet
802.11n (Draft 2.0)	2007	2.4GHz	540Mbps (?)	325 feet (?)

A quick note is necessary about WiFi transmission range. Radio signals don't suddenly stop when they get out of range; they weaken as you get farther away from the transmitter. So an 802.11g network, for example, won't go dead when you get 100 feet distant. Instead, the data transfer rate decreases as the signal decreases. Get 100 or 110 feet away from an 802.11g transmitter, and you're likely to find your transfer rate decreasing from 54Mbps to something approaching 11Mbps. In reality, this gives 802.11g the same (or greater) transmission rate as an 802.11b network, but with no increase in speeds at the further distances.

802.11b

Wi-Fi 802.11b was the first form of Wi-Fi intended for general consumers. Equipment for 802.11b operates in the 2.4GHz RF band and transfers data at a rate of 11 megabits per second (Mbps). Although this is obviously slower than 100Mbps Ethernet, it's more than fast enough for most home and small office uses, especially when compared to a typical 3Mbps (or less) broadband Internet connection.

Several years after the introduction of the original 802.11b equipment, some manufacturers introduced equipment using what they called 802.11b+ technology. This equipment operated in the same 2.4GHz band but transferred data at twice the normal 802.11b rate—22Mbps.

Although you can still find some older 802.11b and 802.11b+ equipment in use, most manufacturers have since upgraded to the newer 802.11g standard.

Network NOTE

The stated data transfer rates for each Wi-Fi protocol are the theoretical maximum. Actual transfer rates typically average half the maximum. This is because wireless devices don't operate in a vacuum; walls, floors, and other obstructions and devices (as well as distance) negatively affect signal strength, and thus the transfer rate.

Network NOTE

How quickly data is transferred across a network is measured in megabits per second, or Mbps. The bigger the Mbps number, the faster the network—and faster is always better than slower.

802.11g

Wi-Fi 802.11g is a newer extension of the Wi-Fi standard. Like the older 802.11b equipment, 802.11g equipment also operates in the 2.4GHz band. This is a faster standard, however, transferring data at a rate of 54Mbps.

Today, some manufacturers sell what they call Extreme G equipment. This equipment upgrades the standard 802.11g firmware to achieve data transfer rates of 108Mbps—twice the normal 802.11g rate. Note, however, that Extreme G equipment from one manufacturer may be incompatible with similar equipment from a different manufacturer, at least at the higher speeds.

802.11a

A common problem with both 802.11b and 802.11g equipment is that these devices often suffer from interference from other devices using the same 2.4GHz RF band, such as baby monitors, cordless phones, and the like. If you experience this type of interference (characterized by dropped signals, slower-than-normal data transfer, and so forth), consider upgrading to 802.11a equipment.

802.11a is an alternate Wi-Fi standard that uses the less-crowded 5.0GHz RF band. This standard makes for reduced interference with other wireless devices while still transferring data at 54Mbps rates.

802.11n and Draft n

The next generation of Wi-Fi, 802.11n, is currently on the drawing boards, with official approval expected sometime in 2007. Although this standard has not yet been finalized, 802.11n is set to deliver faster speeds and a longer range, while remaining backward-compatible with older 802.11b/g systems.

What type of performance will we see from 802.11n systems? Expect transfer rates of at least 200Mbps and possibly up to 540Mbps. Transmission is in the 2.4GHz band, using "smart" multiple in, multiple out (MIMO) antennas and an optional doubling of the frequency spectrum. This should provide not only faster data transfer rates but also an extended transmission range. Whereas current 802.11b and g equipment has a range of about 100 feet between transmitter and receiver, 802.11n promises a range of at least 160 feet, and possibly double that, with less interference from other wireless household devices.

 Network NOTE

In advance of the official 802.11n specification, the Wi-Fi Alliance has certified wireless equipment based on the draft specifications for 802.11n. These products, dubbed "802.11n Draft 2.0 Certified," are guaranteed to be compatible with the final 802.11n specification, which itself is due in 2008. This new certification does not cover previous products manufactured to an earlier draft specification (dubbed "pre-n") that the Wi-Fi Alliance did not certify. You should be safe purchasing "Draft 2.0 Certified" products.

Which Wi-Fi Is the Right Wi-Fi for You?

If you have older Wi-Fi networking equipment, chances are it's of the slower 802.11b variety—which is good, but not great, in terms of speed. When you go shopping for new equipment, you want to go with the newer, faster 80.211g standard—or, if you can buy all your equipment from the same manufacturer, Extreme G or "pre-n" technology. All 802.11g equipment should be fully compatible with older equipment running the 802.11b standard.

If you experience interference with other wireless devices, you should consider moving to 802.11a equipment. These products are just as fast as 802.11g products but operate in the 5.0GHz band for reduced interference.

You should also consider equipment certified to the 802.11n (Draft 2.0) specification. While more expensive, this newer equipment should be at least four times as fast as current equipment—and with a longer range. Newer is always better!

Next: How Windows Vista Handles Wireless Networking

Windows Vista is a significant improvement over Windows XP in many ways, most notably in the area of networking. Just what are these improvements—and how, in general, does networking work with Vista? These questions and more are covered in Chapter 3, "How Windows Vista Handles Wireless Networking." Read on to learn more.

In this chapter

3

How Windows Vista Handles Wireless Networking

Each new version of Windows has made significant improvements in the operating system's networking capabilities. Back in the days of Windows 95 and Windows 98, networking was a complicated affair for technical experts only; you could set up and configure a network from within Windows, but it took a lot of work. Things got much better with Windows XP, where networking became more or less a plug-and-play operation—albeit one that required a lot of user interaction and didn't always work as promised.

With Windows Vista, things again have changed for the better. Microsoft completely rewrote the networking stack in Vista, which means that networking not only is more reliable, it's also much easier to set up. In fact, in most instances you don't have to do much setup at all; Windows Vista recognizes your network and equipment, and automatically configures the system as necessary. (At least theoretically; networking in Vista can still be counterintuitive at times, and occasionally things don't work quite as promised.)

This is good news if you're setting up a new network for your Vista-based computers—but also useful if you're connecting a Vista PC to an existing network or Wi-Fi hot spot.

Vista's New Networking Features

Let's start by taking a look at all the new networking features you'll find in Windows Vista. What's nice about most of these features is that they put a user-friendly front end on what used to be a highly technical process; there's less technical jargon and fewer detailed configuration settings to deal with.

Setting Up a Wireless Network

For most users, the first exposure to Windows Vista networking comes when you set up a new network. Unlike in past versions of Windows, this is done almost completely automatically. In fact, if you have a wired (Ethernet) network, you don't have to do much of anything; Windows' Link Layer Topology Discovery (LLTD) technology automatically detects any connected computers in a network or work-group and then configures the appropriate settings.

To set up a wireless network, Vista includes a new Set Up a Wireless Router or Access Point Wizard, shown in Figure 3.1. This wizard not only helps you configure your wireless router, it also sets up file and printer sharing, creates a private network, and then saves the network settings for you to use to configure other computers on your network.

FIGURE 3.1

Use Vista's Set Up a Wireless Router or Access Point Wizard to quickly and easily set up your new wireless network.

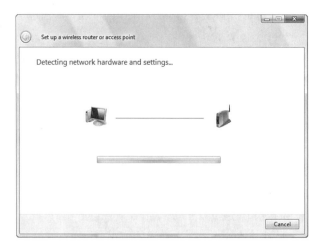

And, as easy as Vista networking is to set up, all those technical settings are still there if you need to access them (via the Network and Sharing Center, which we'll discuss later in this chapter). This way Windows Vista networking appeals to both the typical home computer user and experienced networking professionals.

Windows Connect Now Technology

Setting up additional computers on your network is made easier thanks to Vista's new Windows Connect Now (WCN) technology. This feature lets you save the network settings from your main computer to a USB flash drive. You can then insert the USB drive into any other computer on your network, as shown in Figure 3.2, and it automatically reads the data and configures itself as necessary to work with your new network.

FIGURE 3.2

Windows Connect Now technology lets you transfer network settings from one computer to another using a USB flash drive.

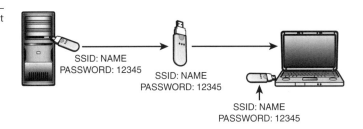

SSID: NAME
PASSWORD: 12345

SSID: NAME
PASSWORD: 12345

SSID: NAME
PASSWORD: 12345

Network and Sharing Center

In previous versions of Windows, you had to open the Windows Control Panel and access a variety of configuration utilities to manage your computer network. Network management is easier under Windows Vista, where the home base for all networking activities is the Network and Sharing Center, shown in Figure 3.3. From here, you can navigate to any computer on your network, set up a new network, troubleshoot network-related problems, and otherwise manage your Windows network.

The first thing you see in the Network and Sharing Center window is a visual representation of that part of your network to which this computer is connected, in the form of a partial network map. You can view a more complete map of your entire network, like the one shown in Figure 3.4, by clicking the View Full Map link. In both instances, you see all the computers connected to your network, including your network router and wireless devices. This lets you grasp in a glance exactly how your network is set up.

Network NOTE

To open the Network and Sharing Center, open the Start menu and select Network. When the Network Explorer opens, click the Network and Sharing Center button.

FIGURE 3.3
The home
base for
Windows Vista
networking—the
Network and
Sharing Center.

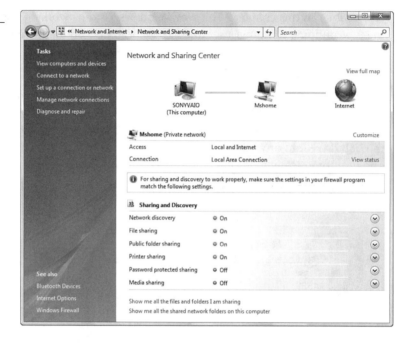

FIGURE 3.4
A full network
map in Windows
Vista.

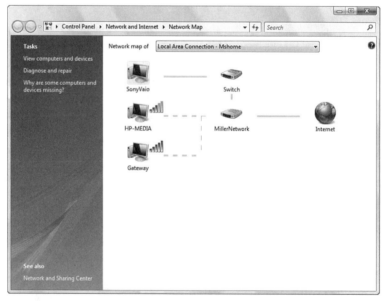

To view the current status of your network—whether it's connected, the connection speed, current activity, and so forth—click the View Status link in the Network and Sharing Center window. This opens the Status window for the network, as shown in Figure 3.5, with appropriate data displayed.

FIGURE 3.5

The Status window for a Windows Vista network.

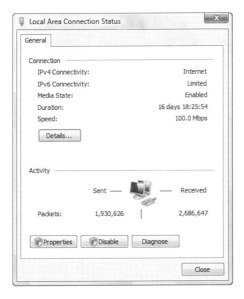

If you're having problems with your network, you can click the Diagnose button in this dialog box to troubleshoot any network problems. Or, if you're a network professional, click the Properties button to access more detailed network configuration options.

Other network-related functions are also accessible from the Network and Sharing Center. Click the appropriate links to manage file and folder sharing, printer sharing, and the like. As I said, this window is the control center for all of Windows Vista's networking operations.

Network Explorer

If you wanted to access other network resources with Windows XP, you accessed the My Network Places window. With Windows Vista, all your networked computers and shared folders are displayed in the new Network Explorer, shown in Figure 3.6.

You can use the Network Explorer to browse content on any connected computer or device, just as you'd browse folders on your PC. Just double-click an icon to open it or view additional content.

Network NOTE

To open the Network Explorer window, open the Start menu and select Network.

FIGURE 3.6

Accessing network computers and shared folders with the Network Explorer.

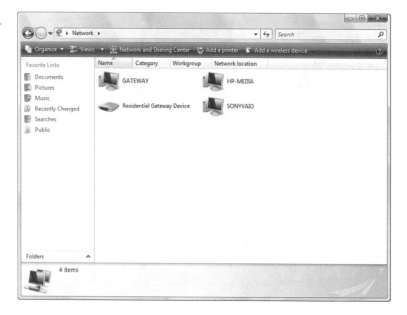

Under the Hood: Vista's Next Generation TCP/IP Stack

As useful as the Network and Sharing Center is, it's not the most important network-related change in Windows Vista. The big news is under the hood, in the technology used to manage all network connections. This technology is called the *TCP/IP stack*, and the one in Vista is completely different from the one used in Windows XP.

The advantage of Vista's new TCP/IP stack (called, appropriately enough, the Next Generation TCP/IP stack), is that it is more robust and more reliable. This makes for more secure and more solid network connections. If you've ever experienced a flaky network connection, or had a computer that wasn't always recognized by the network, you'll appreciate how Vista's Next Generation TCP/IP stack eliminates most of these pesky network connection problems. Vista is, for both networking professionals and the average home user, a much better networking solution than Windows XP or previous versions of the operating system.

You'll notice the Next Generation TCP/IP stack at work the next time you have to set up a network connection or connect to a wireless Internet hot spot. Unlike in past versions of Windows, where establishing a new connection was somewhat tedious and often tenuous, Windows Vista networking is smooth as silk and steady as a rock. You'll experience fewer (if any) dropped connections, and find it much easier to identify and connect with a Wi-Fi hot spot while roaming.

This improved networking is due to several changes that Microsoft engineered into the Next Generation TCP/IP stack. These improvements include

- Support of the newer, more reliable TCP/IP Version 6 standard, along with continued support for the older TCP/IP Version 4.

- A *Quality Windows Audio/Video Experience (qWave)* subsystem to support simultaneous audio/video and data streams that take best advantage of available network bandwidth.

- *Routing compartments* that isolate different networking sessions; this lets you connect to more than one network at a time while maintaining data security between networks.

- *Compound TCP* to provide better performance over high latency connections.

- A *reduction in the number of dropped packets* associated with interference, distance issues, and the like with wireless networks.

In addition, Windows Vista's improved Link Layer Topology Discovery technology makes it easier to find new wireless hot spots, and the new network management features help you save these network settings and manage them as permanent connections. The use of the new Public profile also provides security precautions (such as automatically turning off file sharing) that make your computer data less vulnerable in public situations.

Network NOTE

Learn more about connecting to wireless hot spots in Chapter 14, "Connecting to Wi-Fi Hot Spots and Public Networks."

The bottom line? Vista networks are faster, more reliable, more secure, and easier to configure. If you rely heavily on your computer network, connect to a lot of public Wi-Fi hot spots, or have had networking problems in the past, this improved networking is a major reason to consider upgrading your computers to Windows Vista.

Easier File and Folder Sharing

On a practical basis, Windows Vista also makes it easier to share files and folders over your home or small business network. The file/folder sharing process is not only easier in Vista than it was with Windows XP, it's also more secure.

To share a folder in Windows XP, you had to right-click the folder, select Sharing, and then configure the appropriate settings in the Properties dialog box. You could, with a little effort, enable sharing, give a name to the shared folder, and specify users or groups that could access the share. Everything you needed to do was there, but it seemed a bit Byzantine for the casual user.

The sharing process is a lot easier and easier to understand in Windows Vista. When you right-click a folder and select Share, you now see a new dialog box, shown in Figure 3.7, which walks you through all available folder-sharing options. You decide which users can access the shared folder and what permission level each user has. It's that easy, and in plain English.

FIGURE 3.7

Configuring a shared folder in Windows Vista.

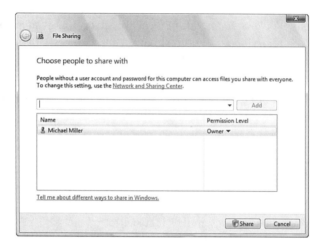

Even easier, you can simply use Vista's Public folder to house the documents you want to share. Any file you copy to the Public folder (located at C:\Users\Public\ on your hard disk) can be viewed, edited, or deleted by other network users, no special configuration necessary.

If you want to limit access to your shared or Public folders, you can use Vista's new password-protected sharing feature. You access this feature from the Network and Sharing Center, as shown in Figure 3.8; when activated, only those network users who have a username and password on the current PC can access shared files and folders. This adds a nice layer of security to your shared documents—especially if you have multiple users using your network.

FIGURE 3.8

Activating password-protected sharing from the Network and Sharing Center.

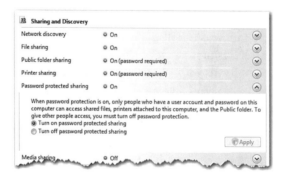

Next: Designing Your Wireless Network

Now that you know how wireless networks work and how Windows Vista handles wireless networking, it's time to start laying out your own network. What should your new network look like, and what equipment do you need? That's what you'll learn in Chapter 4, "Designing Your Wireless Network—And Choosing Network Equipment." Find out more when you turn the page.

In this chapter

- Planning Your Network
- Creating Your Network Equipment List
- Choosing the Right Equipment
- Equipment Buying Tips

4

Designing Your Wireless Network—And Choosing Network Equipment

You don't have to know how wireless networks work to set up your own home or small business network. You do need to know, however, what your network should look like—and what equipment you'll need.

Planning Your Network

Let's start by thinking through just what you need your network to look like. That's right, we're talking network planning—which is actually quite easy.

Making a List

The first step is to list all the devices that you want to connect to the network. I'll make this step a little easier by providing a checklist you can use; just copy the checklist and note which and how many of these devices you currently own.

For example, you might have two desktop computers, one notebook computer, a broadband Internet connection, two printers (one inkjet and one color photo printer), a scanner, and an Xbox 360 video game console. Write down all those devices that you intend to connect to your network.

Mapping the Network

The next step is to take all of these devices, add a network router, and then draw a simple map of how these devices will be connected. You want to distinguish between the following:

- Devices that must be connected to each other via Ethernet cable
- Devices that must be connected to each other via USB cable—that is, those that must be in physical proximity to each other
- Devices that will connect to the network wirelessly

At this point, some explanation is in order.

The first type of device, one that must connect to another via Ethernet cable, might seem out of place in a wireless network. Although it's true that every computer on a wireless network can connect to the network router wirelessly, you might not want to go *completely* wireless. To take full advantage of your router's configuration options and wireless security, one computer needs to connect directly to the router via Ethernet, at least during the setup process. After the initial setup and configuration you can disconnect the Ethernet cable and go wireless for that PC, but for most users it's just as convenient to place the router next to this PC and leave the Ethernet cable connected.

The second type of device is typically a peripheral, such as a printer or scanner that physically connects to a single computer on the network via USB. That is, the peripheral doesn't connect to the network wirelessly; it connects to a computer, which can then make its own wireless connection to the network.

The third type of device is any notebook or desktop computer that is not physically connected to the network router. This type of device has to connect to the network wirelessly.

NETWORK DEVICE CHECKLIST

Quantity	Devices
_____	Desktop computers
_____	Notebook computers
_____	Internet connection (modems)
_____	Printers
_____	Scanners
_____	Network drives (external hard disks)
_____	Video game consoles
_____	Other peripherals:

With this information in hand, sketch out a rough diagram of your network. For the wired connections, you'll want to follow this general flowchart:

Internet connection > Modem > Wireless router > Desktop computer

All other computers should connect to the network wirelessly; make sure you note those peripherals that connect (via USB) to a given wired or wireless PC.

Network NOTE

Some devices, such as notebook PCs, can connect either wired or wirelessly. You need to determine how you want to connect these wired/wireless devices, and plan accordingly.

As an example, the map for a two-desktop, one-laptop, two-printer, one-scanner network should look like the one in Figure 4.1.

FIGURE 4.1

A network map for a three-computer, two-printer network.

Scanner   Desktop PC#3

Printer   Desktop PC#1

Cable Modem   Cable Outlet

Printer   Laptop PC#2

Note, however, that not every network looks the same. For example, if your network consists of a single notebook PC, Internet connection, and printer, the map looks like the one in Figure 4.2.

FIGURE 4.2

A network map for a one-computer, one-printer network.

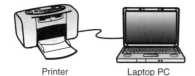

Printer

Laptop PC

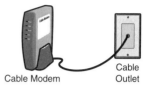

Cable Modem

Cable Outlet

Adding the Necessary Network Equipment

With the first iteration of your network map in hand, you now need to notate the network equipment necessary to implement the network. You've already included one piece of network equipment—the wireless router. Now you need to add the rest of the equipment, as follows:

- Wireless router—One for the entire network.

- Wi-Fi adapters—One for each desktop PC that connects wirelessly. (Such an adapter can be either internal or external—we'll discuss both later in this chapter.)

- Wi-Fi adapter cards—One for each notebook PC that connects wireless and does not have built-in Wi-Fi capability.

- Network interface cards—One for your main desktop PC (if it doesn't have built-in Ethernet capability), and one each for any other PC you want to connect directly to your network router.

- Ethernet cables—One to connect between your main desktop PC and your wireless router, another to connect between your broadband modem and the wireless router, and additional cables for any other PC you want to connect directly to the router.

Network NOTE

Wi-Fi adapters for desktop PCs can be either internal (via a card inserted into your system unit) or external (typically connecting via USB). We'll discuss both types of adapters later in this chapter.

Network NOTE

Most notebook PCs sold today have built-in Wi-Fi capability, and thus do not need auxiliary Wi-Fi adapter cards. If you're not sure as to your notebook's wireless capability, check in your manufacturer's instruction manual, or open the Windows Device Manager look in the Network Adapters section for an installed wireless.

For example, our two desktop/one notebook system will require the following network equipment: one wireless router, one Wi-Fi adapter (for the second desktop), one network interface card (for the main desktop), and two Ethernet cables (for the main desktop and the broadband modem). Figure 4.3 shows the network map with this equipment added.

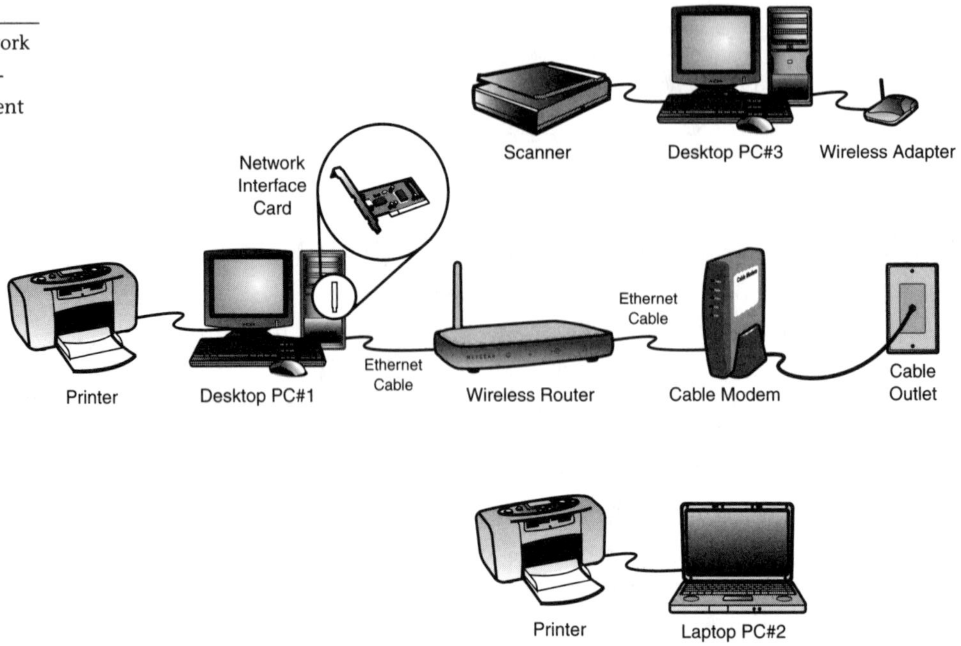

FIGURE 4.3

Our first network map with network equipment added.

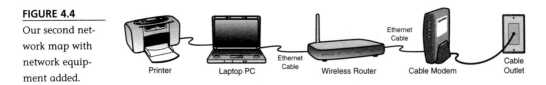

In contrast, our one notebook system requires only the wireless router and two Ethernet cables—one to connect the notebook to the router (for initial setup only) and another to connect the modem to the router. (Figure 4.4 shows this network map with this equipment added.) Because the notebook, like most notebook PCs, has built-in Wi-Fi and Ethernet capability, no additional Wi-Fi adapter or Ethernet card is necessary.

FIGURE 4.4

Our second network map with network equipment added.

Exploring Network Options

The networks discussed so far are fairly traditional, composed of computers, printers, an Internet connection, and a wireless router, all connected together in typical fashion. For your network, however, you might want to consider some variations on the theme.

Combination Modem/Router

Some cable and DSL Internet service providers (ISPs) offer their own proprietary networking equipment to their customers. Having your ISP supply your networking equipment can be attractive, especially if the equipment is offered at low or no cost.

Obviously, your ISP supplies you with a broadband modem; the modem sits between the Internet connection and your computer, modulating and demodulating the digital Internet signal into a format that your computer understands. In a typical network, you connect this modem to your wireless router (not directly to your PC) via an Ethernet or USB cable.

Some ISPs combine the broadband modem and a wireless router into a single modem/router device, such as the one shown in Figure 4.5. Many users like this combination device, sometimes called a *gateway*, because the one unit replaces two pieces of equipment. It also simplifies the hookup and configuration to some degree; you don't have to worry about the router not recognizing or working with the modem, for example. And many of these gateway units include a built-in hardware firewall, which increases your network and Internet security.

FIGURE 4.5

Netgear's DG632 ADSL modem router, used by many DSL service providers.

If you have the option of using a modem/router gateway, you don't have to buy a separate wireless router. Instead, connect the gateway to your Internet connection and then (via Ethernet cable) to your main desktop PC, as shown in Figure 4.6. All your other PCs will connect to the gateway wirelessly.

Wireless Print Server

In most instances, you connect your printer to one of the computers on your network; all your other network PCs access the printer via the connected PC. This type of connection is easy to do and works just fine but is problematic if you can't physically place your printer next to a PC.

Take, for example, our second network map, with a single notebook PC and a printer. What do you do if you want to use your notebook in the bedroom, while your printer remains in your office? With your notebook gone, there's no PC for your printer to connect to.

FIGURE 4.6
A network that uses a combination modem/router gateway device.

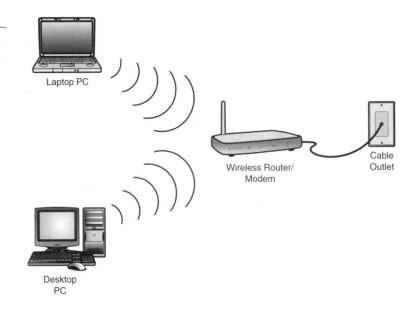

Laptop PC

Wireless Router/
Modem

Cable
Outlet

Desktop
PC

The answer is a piece of networking equipment called a *wireless print server*. This is a small box that connects physically to your printer and wirelessly to your network. With such a print server device, you don't need to connect your printer to a computer; the print server makes all the necessary network connections.

With a wireless print server connected, your network becomes more flexible. Figure 4.7 reflects our working network with a print server added.

Network Extender

Finally, if your house is really big, you may have trouble receiving the signal from your wireless router in outlying rooms. That's because 802.11g equipment has a range of only about 100 feet. This range gets even shorter when the Wi-Fi signal has to go through walls, ceilings, and such. (Radio waves don't turn corners.)

So if the straight-line distance from your wireless router to your farthest PC is more than 60-70 feet or so (horizontally or vertically), consider adding a network extender device, such as the one shown in Figure 4.8. This is essentially a "repeater" antenna that takes the Wi-Fi signal and bounces it farther down the line. The extender does not physically connect to any computer; it only needs AC power and to be in range of the main wireless router.

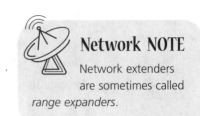

Network NOTE
Network extenders are sometimes called *range expanders.*

FIGURE 4.7

A network that uses a wireless print server for the printer connection.

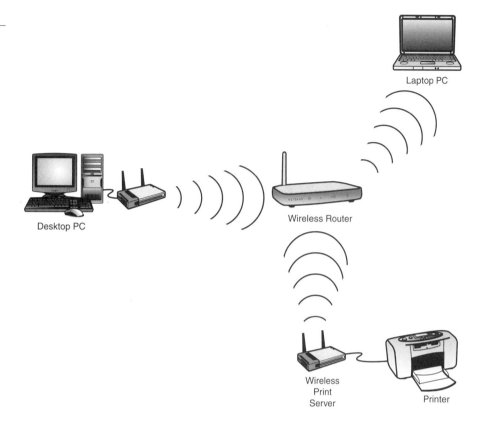

Laptop PC

Desktop PC

Wireless Router

Wireless Print Server

Printer

FIGURE 4.8

The Linksys WRE54G Wireless-G range expander—use to extend the range of your wireless network.

When you add an extender to your network, your network map changes to look like the one in Figure 4.9.

FIGURE 4.9

A network in a larger house that requires the use of a wireless extender.

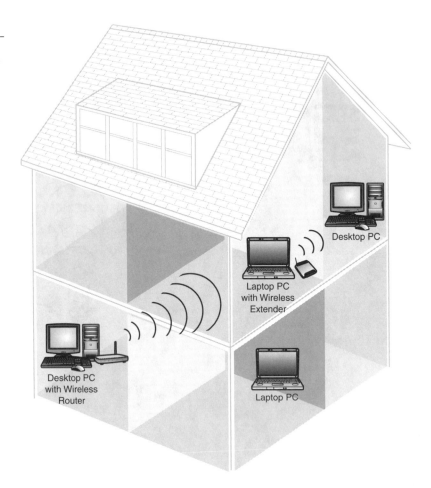

Desktop PC

Laptop PC with Wireless Extender

Desktop PC with Wireless Router

Laptop PC

Creating Your Network Equipment List

With your network properly mapped out, you now need to make a list of the network equipment you need to buy. Work through the equipment you just added to the network map, and write it all down. You can use the following checklist:

Network NOTE

Why the USB memory drive on the network equipment list? It's there to help you transfer network settings from your main PC to all the other PCs on your network, as you'll learn in Chapter 6, "Configuring and Managing Your Network Computers."

NETWORK EQUIPMENT LIST

Quantity	Equipment
_____	Wireless router
_____	Wireless adapters (external, for desktop PCs)
_____	Wireless adapter cards (internal, for desktop PCs)
_____	Wireless adapter cards (for notebook PCs)
_____	Network interface cards (for desktop PCs)
_____	Ethernet cables
_____	Network extender(s)
_____	Wireless print server(s)
_____	USB flash memory drive

Choosing the Right Equipment

Now that you know what equipment you need, it's time to start shopping. There are many different options available, in terms of equipment configuration, functionality, and price. We'll look at each type of equipment separately.

Wireless Router

The central point of any Wi-Fi network is the wireless router, sometimes called a *hub* or *base station*. The wireless router provides several key functions for your network:

- Creates the wireless Wi-Fi network
- Serves as a Wi-Fi hot spot to share your Internet connection wirelessly
- Routes signals and data from one network PC to another
- Offers several Ethernet ports to connect computers directly (nonwirelessly) to the device
- Provides firewall functionality to protect your network from outside attack

One important point is that a wireless router, while providing wireless network connections, also provides *wired* network connections. As you can see in Figure 4.10, most wireless routers have at least four Ethernet connections on the back; you'll use one of these to connect your broadband modem, but the rest are open to connect any network computer via Ethernet cable.

FIGURE 4.10

The connections on the back of the D-Link DI-624 wireless router— one Ethernet connector for a broadband modem, and four to connect to other network PCs.

802.11g Routers

The first decision you have to make when choosing a wireless router is which Wi-Fi protocol you want to use. As you recall from Chapter 2, "How Wireless Networks Work," three primary types of Wi-Fi equipment are in use today: 802.11b, 802.11g, and 802.11a.

The "b" equipment is mainly older, supporting the slower 11Mbps standard. The "a" equipment uses a different frequency range (5.0GHz), which has less interference with other household devices, but as such is incompatible with non-a Wi-Fi equipment.

This leaves the "g" equipment, which is the current standard—to a point. Wi-Fi 802.11g equipment operates in the common 2.4GHz frequency range, at speeds of up to 54Mbps. And, just in case you have some older networking equipment in your network, a "g" router is fully compatible with older "b" devices. You'll find 802.11g routers from all the major network equipment manufacturers, including Belkin, D-Link, Linksys, and Netgear; expect to pay from $50 to $80. (Figure 4.11 shows a typical 802.11g wireless router, from Linksys.)

Network NOTE

There are two reasons why you might want or need to connect a computer via Ethernet to a wireless modem. First, you'll need to connect your main desktop PC via Ethernet to access the router's configuration settings. Second, Ethernet is faster than Wi-Fi, so if you need faster data transmission (for large files or real-time gaming), Ethernet is the way to go.

Network NOTE

You may want to consider 802.11a equipment (both router and wireless adapter) if you get a lot of interference with other electronic devices. You can buy pure 802.11a routers, or dual a/g routers that offer both 802.11a and 802.11g transmission and reception—and are compatible with any 802.11g devices you might have on your network.

FIGURE 4.11

The Linksys WRT54G 802.11g wireless router.

Extreme G Routers

That said, 802.11g is not the fastest equipment on the market today. Most networking companies sell so-called Extreme G equipment, which doubles the speed of an 802.11g network from 54Mbps to 108Mbps. You get this speed boost when you pair an Extreme G router with Extreme G wireless adapters; connecting a standard 802.11g adapter to an Extreme G router results in the default 54Mbps 802.11g connection speed for the "regular G" computer.

All the major manufacturers offer various types of Extreme G routers; expect to pay from $70 to $100. (Figure 4.12 shows a typical Extreme G wireless router from Netgear.)

Network NOTE

Don't get confused by conflicting terminology. D-Link calls its Extreme G technology Xtreme G or Wireless 108G. Linksys calls its Extreme G technology SpeedBooster. Netgear calls its Extreme G technology Super-G. Whatever the brand name, it's the same technology.

FIGURE 4.12

The Netgear WGT624 Super-G wireless router.

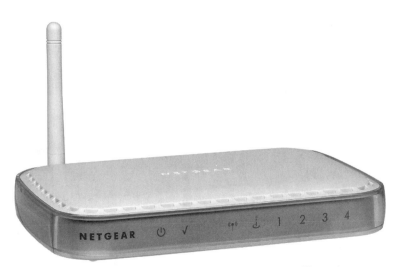

802.11n (Draft 2.0) Routers

Another option is to go with equipment certified to the 802.11n (Draft 2.0) specification. This equipment is compatible with the latest draft of the 802.11n protocol—as well as with all older 802.11 protocols.

That said, 802.11n equipment is up to 10 times faster than 802.11g equipment, with maximum

Network NOTE

All 802.11n equipment should be fully backward compatible with existing 802.11b and g equipment. An 802.11n router should work just fine with a 802.11g wireless adapter—but at 802.11g speeds.

speeds approaching 540Mbps. (Actual speeds will most likely be in the 200–250Mbps range.) Even better, 802.11n equipment promises up to four times the range of standard 802.11g equipment—assuming you pair an 802.11n router with an 802.11n wireless adapter, of course.

Again, all the manufacturers are jumping on the 802.11n bandwagon; expect to pay from $100 to $200 for a 802.11n router. (Figure 4.13 shows a typical 802.11n router, from Belkin.)

FIGURE 4.13

Belkin's F5D8230 wireless pre-N router—note the multiple antennas for greater range.

Wireless Adapters

Next, you'll need to purchase wireless adapters for any computer that doesn't have built-in Wi-Fi capability. The adapter is the miniature transmitter/receiver that connects your PC to your network's wireless router.

Naturally, you have to choose between 802.11a, 802.11g, Extreme G, and 802.11n adapters; you should buy the same type of adapter as you do the router. Then you can select a specific type of adapter, based on the type of computer you have.

Network TIP

You can also connect any external wireless adapter to a notebook PC, instead of using an adapter card. The best type of unit for this purpose is the keychain USB wireless adapter, which is small enough to fit in your pocket when not in use.

External Adapters for Desktop PCs

If you're connecting a desktop PC, the most popular type of wireless adapter is the external type, which connects via USB to your computer. There are actually two different physical configurations for this type of adapter: External units, such as the one in Figure 4.14, that connect via a short USB cable, and keychain units, such as the one in Figure 4.15, that are small enough to fit on a keychain and plug directly into your PC's USB port, no cable required.

Depending on the brand, configuration, and functionality, expect to pay between $40 and $100 for an external wireless adapter.

FIGURE 4.14

Linksys's WUSB54G full-size external Wireless-G USB network adapter.

FIGURE 4.15

D-Link's DWL-G122 keychain wireless USB adapter.

Internal Adapters for Desktop PCs

If you don't want an external wireless adapter cluttering your desktop, you can always use an internal unit. This is a wireless adapter on an internal card, such as the one in Figure 4.16, that you install inside your PC's system unit. For optimal reception, these cards have either an antenna sticking out the back or an external antenna on a short cable.

There are two downsides to using an internal wireless adapter card. First, you have to open up your PC's system unit and install the thing, which might be somewhat daunting to the technically inexperienced user. Second, this type of configuration typically places the Wi-Fi antenna low to the ground, which might not provide optimal reception. For these reasons, I usually recommend an external adapter over the internal type.

FIGURE 4.16

Belkin's F5D7000 Wireless G desktop card.

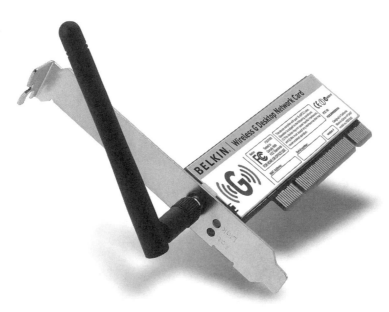

If you decide to go with an internal wireless adapter card, expect to pay between $35 and $90.

Adapter Cards for Notebook PCs

If you happen to own a notebook PC that doesn't have built-in Wi-Fi capability (and they're pretty rare), there are two ways to add this capability—you can connect an external wireless adapter or insert a wireless adapter card. This is a different kind of card from the internal card you use with desktop PCs; as you can see in Figure 4.17, this type of adapter inserts into your notebook's PC Card slot and adds automatic Wi-Fi functionality. Expect to pay $50 to $100 for a PC Card adapter.

Network Interface Cards (NICs)

Although it's possible to set up a wireless network with no Ethernet connections, it's not recommended. That's because you need a direct nonwireless connection between your main PC and your network router to both configure the router and enable wireless security functions; most wireless routers don't let you do configuration wirelessly. Also, as I mentioned earlier in this chapter, if you do a lot of intensive web surfing, online game playing or any other bandwidth hogging activity, you'll be much happier doing that over Ethernet.

Knowing this, it's important that at least one PC on your network have either built-in Ethernet capability or an installed network interface card (NIC). If your main PC isn't Ethernet-capable, you'll have to purchase and install a NIC for that computer; these cards are typically priced from $30 to $50.

FIGURE 4.17

Netgear's WG511 wireless PC Card.

As you can see in Figure 4.18, a network interface card is like any other card you install in your PC's system unit. You turn off your PC, unplug the power cable, open up the case, and insert the card into an open slot on the computer's motherboard. When you button up the case and turn your computer back on, you'll need to install the software that came with the NIC. After the NIC is installed, you can plug any Ethernet cable into the card's Ethernet connector.

FIGURE 4.18

The Linksys LNE100TX EtherFast 10/100 LAN Card.

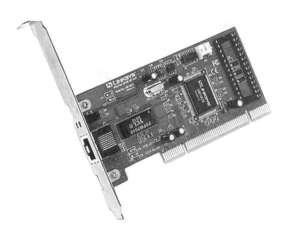

By the way, most notebook PCs have built-in Ethernet capability. To add Ethernet to a non-Ethernet notebook, you can use an Ethernet PC Card (such as the one in Figure 4.19) or an external Ethernet adapter (such as the one in Figure 4.20), which connects to your notebook via USB. You can also use an external USB Ethernet adapter with a desktop PC; if you have a free USB port, it's easier than installing an internal card. Expect to pay from $30 to $50 for an Ethernet PC Card, or from $30 to $60 for an external Ethernet-to-USB adapter.

Network NOTE

Many Ethernet cards are billed as 10/100. This means that they're capable of Fast Ethernet's 100Mbps transmission rate but can also operate at the slower speed if connected to a 10Mbps hub.

FIGURE 4.19

The D-Link DGE-660TD GigaExpress gigabit Ethernet PC Card.

FIGURE 4.20

The Linksys USB100M 10/100 EtherFast compact USB adapter.

When purchasing a NIC or external Ethernet adapter, your main choice is speed. There are actually three different Ethernet standards, based on data transmission speed. The oldest standard, 10Base-T, transmits data at a paltry 10Mbps. More common is 100Base-T or Fast Ethernet, which transmits data at 100Mbps. Even faster is Gigabit Ethernet, which supports transmission speeds of up to 1Gbps (that's one billion bits per second). You should probably purchase the fastest card or adapter that fits within your budget.

Ethernet Cable

To connect your Ethernet-capable PC and your broadband modem to your network router, you'll need to use Ethernet cables. Ethernet cables, such as the one in Figure 4.21, are thick cables with connectors that look like slightly oversized telephone connectors. You'll pay between $10 and $20 for a 10- or 25-foot cable; you probably don't need a really long one.

Wi-Fi Extender

As discussed earlier in this chapter, if your wireless network is in a large house or office, you may need a Wi-Fi extender to add the necessary range to your wireless transmissions. Most extenders, such as the one in Figure 4.22, run from $70 to $150, and are available from all major networking equipment manufacturers. Setup is typically no more complex than connecting it to a power source and turning it on; the repeater functionality should work seamlessly with most routers.

Network CAUTION
Make sure your Wi-Fi extender matches the Wi-Fi protocol used by your wireless router. You don't want to use a 802.11g extender with a pre-N router.

FIGURE 4.21

A typical Ethernet cable, from Linksys.

FIGURE 4.22

Belkin's F5D7132 Wireless-G universal range extender.

Wireless Print Server

Finally, the last piece of equipment you may want to consider is the wireless print server, as discussed earlier in this chapter. You use a wireless print server to connect your printer to your network without having to first connect it to a PC.

Wireless print servers, such as the one in Figure 4.23, are typically priced from $100 to $150. Setup, unfortunately, is often quite complex, and you may

Network CAUTION

Many older wireless print servers do not work with multifunction printers—printers that also offer fax and copying functions. You'll want to choose a newer model with multifunction printer support, such as the D-Link DPR-1260 Rangebooster G Multifunction Print Perver.

run into compatibility issues. For that reason, it might be wise to choose a wireless print server by the same manufacturer as your wireless router.

FIGURE 4.23

D-Link's DPR-1260 Rangebooster G multifunction print server—one of the few devices that work with multifunction printers.

Equipment Buying Tips

With all these different models and features available, how do you choose the right equipment for your wireless network? Here are some tips for shopping smarter:

- For best compatibility with different types of equipment—and the lowest price—stick with 802.11g (*not* Extreme G) equipment. If you go 802.11g, you can mix and match equipment from different manufacturers and be fully compatible with older 802.11b devices.

- For a faster connection, go with Extreme G equipment—but only if all your equipment comes from the same manufacturer. Because Extreme G is not an industrywide standard, units from one manufacturer might not work well with units from another company.

Network TIP

Where can you purchase networking equipment? Just about anywhere that computer equipment is sold. That includes computer stores (CompUSA, Fry's, etc.), office supply stores (Office Depot, Staples, and so on), consumer electronics stores (Best Buy, Circuit City, and the like), and all sorts of online retailers—including Amazon.com. Make sure you shop around for the best prices!

■ For the ultimate wireless performance, consider purchasing equipment certi-fied compatible with the 802.11n (Draft 2.0) specification. When using all 802.11n equipment, expect the fastest possible performance over the longest possible range.

■ In most instances, going with external wireless adapters that connect via USB makes for easier connections. Make sure, however, that you can place the external adapter in a position away from other electrical equipment, to minimize interference and establish a stronger signal. (In this regard, con-necting a keychain Wi-Fi adapter to the rear of a desktop PC often results in disappointing performance.)

In other words, if you go with an established standard, such as 802.11g, you can mix and match wireless equipment from different companies and eras. If you go with a proprietary solution, such as Extreme G, you may not be able to use equip-ment produced by a different manufacturer. Of course, you can always go for 802.11n (Draft 2.0) equipment, which is faster and has a longer range than current equipment—even if it isn't the final 802.11n specification quiet yet.

Next: Setting Up Your Wireless Network

When you get back from the electronics store with your bag full of stuff, you can start setting up your network. This involves a lot of connecting and configuring, as you'll learn in Chapter 5, "Setting Up Your Wireless Network."

Part II

Setting Up Your Wireless Network

In this chapter

5

Setting Up Your Wireless Network

In Chapter 4, "Designing Your Wireless Network—And Choosing Network Equipment," you planned your wireless network and chose the necessary networking equipment. With this equipment in hand, it's now time to physically create your network—get all that equipment set up, connected, and properly configured.

Roll up your sleeves—there's work ahead!

Before You Start

Before you start connecting all your networking equipment, you need to do a little prep work. In particular, you need to assemble everything you need to get things up and running, and perhaps install a networking card in your main desktop PC.

What You Need—And Where to Put It

The first items you need to assemble are all your networking equipment—the network router, wireless adapters, and the like you identified in Chapter 4. Don't connect anything yet, but do place each piece of equipment next to the computer to which it belongs. In the case of your wireless router, place it next to what you consider your main PC—the computer you'll be using to configure the router—and near your broadband Internet modem. (Figure 5.1 shows a typical setup.)

FIGURE 5.1

Place your wireless router next to the main PC and broadband modem.

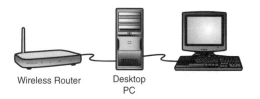

Wireless Router   Desktop PC

Next, because the wireless router requires power, make sure you place it next to a free power outlet—or, even better, next to a surge suppressor power strip. You'll also want to arrange power for any other AC-powered devices, such as a wireless extender or wireless print server. (Network adapters typically don't need AC power, instead receiving their power from the host PC.)

For all the wireless equipment, make sure that each device is relatively out in the open, not buried in a cabinet or behind other equipment, as shown in Figure 5.2. Although Wi-Fi signals can travel through most solid objects, such placement rapidly degrades the signal. It's better to place all equipment where it can be seen, to maximize the signal strength over the necessary distance.

In addition, you probably want to place the wireless router away from other electronic equipment, as shown in Figure 5.3. That means moving it away from your cordless phone, PC, or computer monitor. (Moving just a foot away might be good enough.) Any and all of these devices emit electronic signals that can interfere with the router's radio frequency transmission.

FIGURE 5.2

Don't bury your equipment!

FIGURE 5.3

Avoid close encounters with other electronic equipment.

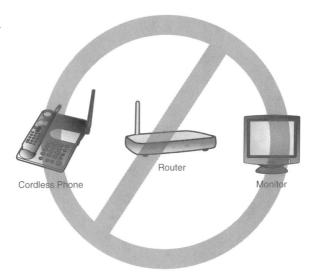

Cordless Phone

Router

Monitor

Finally, make sure you have all necessary cables to complete your network. Although you don't have to deal with many cables in a wireless network (that's one of the advantages, after all), you do need at least two Ethernet cables—one to connect your broadband modem to the wireless router, and another to connect your main PC to the router. Make sure the cables are of adequate length.

What You Might Need to Do: Install a Network Interface Card

At least for initial setup and configuration purposes, you'll need to connect your main PC to your wireless router via an Ethernet cable. If your main PC doesn't have a built-in Ethernet port, you'll need to install an internal network interface card (NIC) or an external Ethernet adapter via USB.

We discussed both these options in Chapter 4, but let's spend a bit more time on the NIC option—in particular, the steps you may need to take to install such a card in your desktop PC.

Installing a network interface card is no different from installing any other type of internal card. Follow these steps:

1. Power down your PC and unplug the power cable.

2. Remove the computer case, as shown in Figure 5.4.

Network CAUTION

You should protect your new card against electrostatic discharge (ESD), caused by a build up of static electricity. To do this, make sure you and your computer are properly grounded. For this purpose, you may want to purchase and wear a special anti-static wrist strap while you're working inside your PC.

FIGURE 5.4

Remove your computer's case.

3. Find a card slot in the PC that is both free and fits your specific network card. Most PCs will have either PCI or PCI-Express (or both). Make sure that you determine which type of slot your PC uses and purchase the correct wireless adapter card.

4. Unscrew the plate that covers the card slot's opening on the rear of the computer and remove the plate, as shown in Figure 5.5. Set the plate and screw aside.

FIGURE 5.5
Remove the plate
that covers the
open card slot.

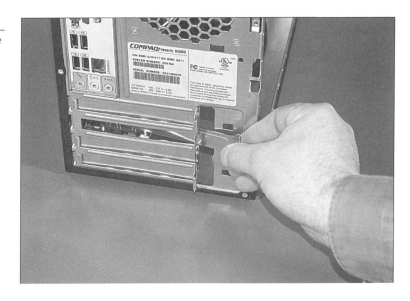

5. Align the card with the slot in the PC and push gently but firmly to seat the card in its slot, as shown in Figure 5.6.

FIGURE 5.6
Insert the net-
work card
into the open
card slot.

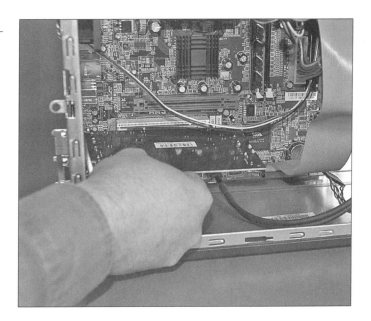

6. Using the screw that you set aside in step 4, screw the card in to hold it in place, as shown in Figure 5.7.

FIGURE 5.7

Secure the
network card
into place.

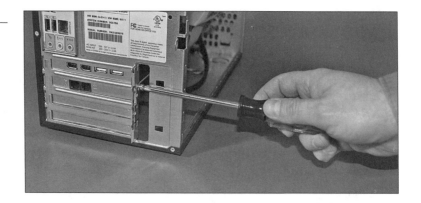

7. Replace the computer case.

8. Reconnect the computer's power cable and
   power up your PC.

9. Run the installation software that came
   with the network card to install the drivers
   for the card. (You may also want to check
   with the manufacturer's website to see if
   updated drivers are available for the card.)

After the card is properly installed, you can connect an Ethernet cable to the jack on the rear of
the card—and proceed with your network setup.

Network TIP

Instead of installing
an internal network card, many
users find it far easier to use an
external Ethernet adapter. This
type of adapter connects to any
open USB port, either directly or
via a short cable.

Connecting Your Broadband Modem to the Wireless Router

Now it's time to start connecting things. The first item we'll connect is the broadband modem you use to connect to the Internet. Follow these steps:

1. Make sure your broadband modem is connected both to a power source and
   to your incoming Internet connection, and that it is powered on.

2. Place the wireless router near the broadband modem, but do not yet connect
   it to a power source.

3. Connect one end of an Ethernet cable to the Ethernet out port on your
   broadband modem, as shown in Figure 5.8.

4. Connect the other end of the Ethernet cable to one of the Ethernet ports on
   your wireless router, as shown in Figure 5.9. (Many routers have a dedicated
   port for the modem connection, often labeled "Internet" or something similar; if so, use this port.)

FIGURE 5.8

Connect an
Ethernet cable to
your broadband
modem.

FIGURE 5.9

Connect the other
end of the
Ethernet cable to
your wireless
router.

Do not plug in or power up your wireless router just yet. There's more connecting to
do before you power it up.

Connecting Your Main Computer to the Wireless Router

With your broadband modem connected, you can now proceed to connect your main PC to the wireless router. Your PC should already be powered up and running; the router, not so.

Setting Up the Router

To set up your router, you connect it via an Ethernet cable to your main PC. Although it may seem counterintuitive to make a wired connection to a wireless network, there's a reason for this.

Before your router can connect to your PC via wireless signals, the router has to be properly configured for wireless operation. However, you can't configure the router wirelessly if the wireless operation has yet to be configured. (That's a nice Catch-22!) So you have to initially connect your PC to the router via an Ethernet cable, which provides a direct connection to the router. Thus connected, you can work your way through the router's wireless configuration routine. (This routine should also involve the configuration of your network's wireless security, which is discussed in more detail in Chapter 8, "Securing Your Wireless Network.")

After the router is configured, you can disconnect the Ethernet cable and connect your PC to the router wirelessly. You shouldn't have to use the Ethernet connection again—unless you need to change the main configuration at some future date.

Note that some wireless router manufacturers do let you configure the router without first connecting your PC via Ethernet. In some instances, you may be able to establish a basic wireless connection this way, but not enable any wireless security; a physical (Ethernet) connection is required to set the necessary encryption. In any case, make sure you follow the setup instructions provided by your router's manufacturer.

So, to complete the fullest possible setup and configuration of your wireless router, follow these steps:

1. Run the installation software that came with your wireless router. Follow the onscreen instructions to install the necessary software and drivers.

2. When prompted, connect one end of an Ethernet cable to an Ethernet port on your wireless router, as shown in Figure 5.10.

3. Connect the other end of the Ethernet cable to the Ethernet port on your main PC, as shown in Figure 5.11.

4. Connect your wireless router to a power source and, if it has a power switch, turn it on.

5. Your PC should now recognize and automatically install the router.

FIGURE 5.10

Connect an Ethernet cable to your wireless router.

FIGURE 5.11

Connect the other end of the Ethernet cable to your main computer.

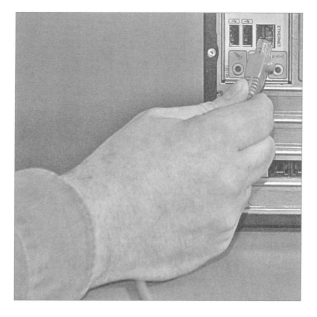

After your PC recognizes and installs the router, you'll probably be prompted by the router's installation software to configure the router; follow the onscreen instructions to do so. You might also be prompted to reboot your computer to complete the installation. If necessary, do this.

Running the Router's Setup Program

What does wireless router installation involve? It all depends on your make and model of router. Every manufacturer does it a bit differently. For example, I recently installed a Netgear Super G wireless router, and here's how the process went:

I started by inserting the router's installation CD into my computer's CD drive. This launched Netgear's Smart Wizard Setup program, shown in Figure 5.12. I clicked the Setup button from the main screen, and then the software started to install. The software checked my current setup, asked me a few questions to determine what type of network I was setting up, and then directed me to connect the various cables in the proper order. With the cables connected, the setup program then told me to connect the power cable and power on the router.

FIGURE 5.12

The Smart Wizard Setup program for a Netgear wireless router.

When the router powered on, the router configuration utility opened in my web browser and automatically detected my Internet connection. I was then prompted to enter an SSID (the default was NETGEAR; you don't want to use the default), and then led through the wireless security setup. I choose WPA security and entered an easily remembered passphrase.

This process completed, the configuration utility displayed the summary screen shown in Figure 5.13. I printed the screen in case I ever need to change these settings in the future; then the utility applied the settings and tested the network.

Fortunately for me, everything worked fine as tests. All in all, it was a painless process with little intervention required on my part.

FIGURE 5.13

The summary
screen for
Netgear's config-
uration utility.
(Wireless Pass-
phrase and
Admin Password
blurred inten-
tionally.)

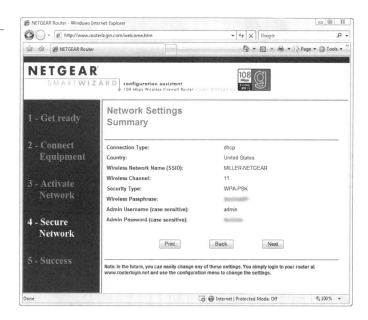

Setting Up Your Wireless Router in Windows

Note that installing the wireless router does not
fully configure your computer for the new wireless
network. It only installs the device drivers and operating software for the router on your main PC—
and, if you opt to, configures wireless security for
the router. After the router is installed, you'll need
to configure the host PC to set up your new network,
which you do via Windows Vista's Set Up a Wireless
Router or Access Point Wizard. That's a separate
operation; turn to Chapter 6, "Configuring and
Managing Your Network Computers," to work
through this process.

Network NOTE

After your wireless
router is configured,
you can leave your main PC
connected to the router via
Ethernet (it's much faster this
way), or you can disconnect the
Ethernet cable and configure
your PC for wireless operation,
using a wireless adapter. If you
go the wireless route, you'll still
need to connect your computer
to the router via Ethernet cable
if you ever want to reconfigure
any of the router's settings.

Connecting Additional Desktop PCs

After you've connected and configured your main PC and wireless router, you can
connect additional PCs to your network. Naturally, each additional PC on your network requires its own wireless adapter; for the purposes of these instructions, we'll
assume you're using an external Wi-Fi adapter on each PC.

Installing a Wireless Adapter

Follow these steps:

1. Run the installation software provided for the wireless adapter.

2. When prompted, connect the wireless adapter to a USB port on the PC, as shown in Figure 5.14. (The adapter doesn't connect to a power outlet; it receives its power from the host PC.)

3. Your PC should now recognize and automatically install the wireless adapter.

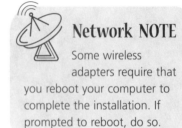

Network NOTE

Some wireless adapters require that you reboot your computer to complete the installation. If prompted to reboot, do so.

FIGURE 5.14

Connect the external wireless adapter to a USB port on your PC.

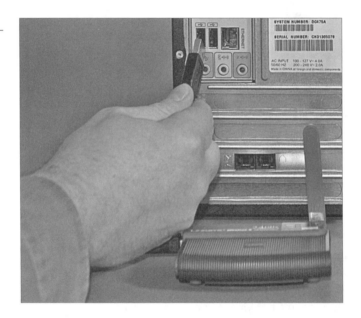

Running the Wireless Adapter Setup Program

As with wireless router setup, every wireless adapter has its own unique installation and configuration routine. This routine is dictated by the installation software that comes with the router; every manufacturer does it a bit differently.

As an example, Figure 5.15 shows the main screen of the Smart Wizard setup program that accompanies a Netgear Super G wireless adapter. When you click the Next button, the necessary software and device drivers are installed; then you're prompted to insert the adapter into an available USB slot on your computer.

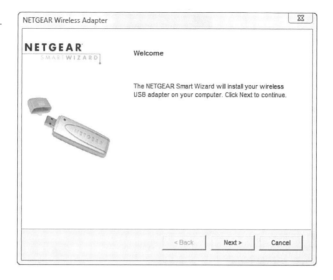

The adapter is installed, but you now have to choose the wireless network to which you want to connect. You do this from within Windows. Open the Start menu and select Connect To; this displays a list of available wireless networks, as shown in Figure 5.16. The list probably includes some of your neighbors' wireless networks, as well as your own. Select your network from the list and click Connect.

As you can see in Figure 5.17, you're now prompted to enter the network key or passphrase that you used to configure your wireless router. Enter the password and then click Connect. When you're connected to the network, click the Close button, and you're ready to go.

FIGURE 5.17

Enter the network key or passphrase for your network.

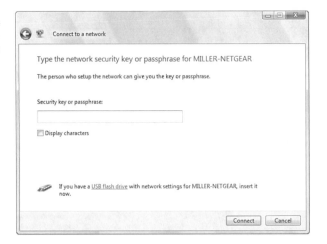

Connecting Notebook PCs

If you have a notebook PC with built-in Wi-Fi networking, you can skip most of this process; your PC's wireless adapter is already there and working.

Instead, all you need to do is make sure that your notebook PC connects to your newly operational wireless network. Follow these steps:

1. Make sure that the Wi-Fi functionality is enabled on your notebook PC. You may have to flip a switch or press a specific key combination to turn on wireless networking.

2. Open the Windows Start menu and select Connect To.

3. Windows now displays the Connect to a Network dialog box, which lists all wireless networks in the immediate vicinity. Select your new network; then click the Connect button.

Windows now connects your computer to your wireless network.

Network TIP

You can also open the Connect to a Network dialog box by right-clicking the wireless network connection icon in the Windows system tray and selecting Connect to a Network.

Network CAUTION

Some wireless adapters, including those built into notebook PCs, default to their own software to configure and manage the adapter's operation. If you click the wireless network connection icon and receive a message to the effect that Windows is not managing this operation, you'll need to launch and use the wireless adapter's software program instead. When in doubt, consult the instruction manual that came with your wireless adapter—or, in the case of a notebook PC, that part of the PC's instruction manual that addresses wireless connection issues.

Setting Your Network Location

The first time you connect a computer to your wireless network, Windows Vista prompts you to set your *network location*. This isn't an actual physical location, but rather describes a type of network—Home, Work, or Public. Each type of network has its own default security settings appropriate to the needs of that network type.

Table 5.1 describes the three network location types.

Table 5.1   Windows Vista Network Location Types

Location	Used For	Public or Private?	Description
Home	Home networks	Private	Enables Network Discovery so you can see other network computers
			Enables file and folder sharing
			Configures the Windows Firewall to allow programs and other communication
Work	Office networks	Private	Enables Network Discovery so you can see other network computers
			Enables file and folder sharing
			Configures the Windows Firewall to allow programs and other communication
Public Place	Wi-Fi hot spots	Public	Disables Network Discovery
			Disables file and folder sharing
			Hides computer name from other nearby computers
			Configures the Windows Firewall to block certain programs and services and protect your PC from unauthorized access

If you're connecting to a home network, choose Home. If you're connecting to a small office network, select Work. (They both use the same settings, for what it's worth.) Choose Public Place only if you're connecting to a public Wi-Fi hot spot, such as those you find at coffeehouses and restaurants.

Connecting Other Network Equipment

After all your computers are connected to your network, you can connect other networking devices as necessary. For example, you may want to connect the following equipment:

- Network printer—Unless you're using a wireless print server (discussed next), network printers connect indirectly to your network, via a previously connected PC. Just connect the printer to the PC as normal, and configure the printer as a shared printer for that computer. You'll then need to install the shared printer on each network PC. (Learn more about network printers in Chapter 12, "Sharing Printers and Other Peripherals.")

- Wireless print server—If you want to share on your network a printer that isn't physically connected to PC, you use a separate piece of equipment called a wireless print server. The wireless print server connects physically to your printer (typically via USB) and wirelessly to your network. Learn more about connecting and using print servers in Chapter 12.

- Wireless network extender—If you have trouble receiving the Wi-Fi signal on computers distant from your wireless router, you can "repeat" the signal using a wireless network extender. Connecting an extender is simplicity itself; just connect it to a power source and turn it on. The extender automatically receives the existing Wi-Fi signal and repeats it, effectively extending the range of the signal.

- Video game device—If you have a new-generation video game console (Microsoft Xbox 360, Nintendo Wii, or Sony PlayStation 3) or a handheld game device with wireless functionality, you can connect that game device to your wireless network. The connection process differs from device to device; learn more in Chapter 13, "Connecting Game Devices to Your Wireless Network."

Next: Configuring Your Network Computers

Physically connecting your network equipment is just the first part of setting up your network. Equally important is setting up the network on each computer, which we'll do in Chapter 6, "Configuring and Managing Your Network Computers." Turn the page to get started.

In this chapter

6

Configuring and Managing Your Network Computers

In the Chapter 5, "Setting Up Your Wireless Network," you learned how to physically connect all the computers and other equipment in your wireless network. Connecting everything is just part of what you need to do, however; you also have to create your new network and properly configure each of your computers to connect to this network.

Fortunately, Windows Vista makes creating and configuring a network much easier than it's been with previous versions of Windows. Assuming your main computer is running Vista, the process is a relative snap.

Configuring Network Computers in Windows Vista

For purposes of this chapter, we'll assume that the computer you have connected to your wireless router is running Windows Vista. The other computers on your network can be running Vista or the older Windows XP; we'll cover both types of configurations. But for setting up the network itself, it's worth moving up to Vista to make the process go much more smoothly.

Setting Up Your Wireless Router

After you connect your wireless router to your main computer (via a handy Ethernet cable), you have to both install the router's drivers and software on the PC and configure the router itself. We covered router installation in Chapter 5; router configuration, however, can be more involved.

You typically access your router's configuration settings via your web browser, entering the address specified in your router's instruction manual. The confusing part is that each router has its own unique configuration routine, all different enough to make it impossible to cover each and every one in detail. (Figure 6.1 shows a configuration page for a Linksys router.)

That said, most router configuration software utilities let you configure the following major options:

FIGURE 6.1

The configuration utility for a Linksys router.

- Network name or SSID (Service Set Identifier)
- Router IP address (This is the same address you used to access the configuration page; a default address is typically given in the router's instruction manual.)
- Username and password (used to access the router configuration utility in the future)
- Wireless security (type of security and the network key or password)

You may also have the option to enable or disable SSID broadcast; this determines whether the network name is publicly broadcast. Disabling SSID broadcast effectively hides your network from most potential attacks. (When the SSID isn't broadcast, outsiders have no easy way to find your network.)

Network NOTE
Learn more about wireless security in Chapter 8, "Securing Your Wireless Network."

Click the Save Settings button to save the configuration settings for the router.

Configuring Windows Vista

Some of these same settings can also be configured within Windows Vista. After you set up your router with its own configuration routine, you'll want to run Vista's new Set Up a Wireless Router or Access Point Wizard. This wizard configures Windows for your wireless router—and also sets various network-related settings for the operating system.

Network NOTE
Windows Vista's Set Up a Wireless Router or Access Point Wizard replaces two separate wizards found in Windows XP—the Network Setup Wizard and the Wireless Network Setup Wizard.

To use this wizard, make sure your computer is connected to your router via Ethernet and follow these steps:

1. Open the Windows Start menu and select Control Panel.
2. From the Control Panel, select Network and Internet; then select Network and Sharing Center.
3. From the Network and Sharing Center, click Set Up a Connection or Network.
4. When the Set Up a Connection or Network window appears, as shown in Figure 6.2, select Set Up a Wireless Router or Access Point and then click Next.
5. When the Set Up a Wireless Router or Access Point Wizard appears, as shown in Figure 6.3, click Next.

FIGURE 6.2

The Set Up a Connection or Network window—the gateway to several network configuration operations.

FIGURE 6.3

The first screen of Windows Vista's Set Up a Wireless Router or Access Point Wizard.

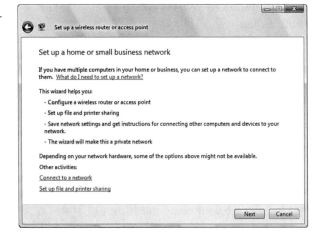

6. Windows now examines your network connections to detect your network hardware and settings, as shown in Figure 6.4.

7. If Windows can complete the setup automatically, it does. Otherwise, it displays the dialog box shown in Figure 6.5. If you want to use your router's configuration utility to complete the setup, select Configure This Device Manually; this launches the configuration utility in a browser window. Otherwise, you can complete the configuration manually by selecting Create Wireless Network Settings and Save to USB Flash Drive.

8. If you chose the second option, you're now asked to give your network a name, as shown in Figure 6.6. What you're doing is assigning an SSID, which can be up to 32 characters long.

FIGURE 6.4

Detecting your network hardware and settings.

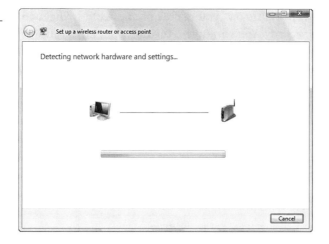

FIGURE 6.5

If you see this window, you can choose to manually complete the configuration.

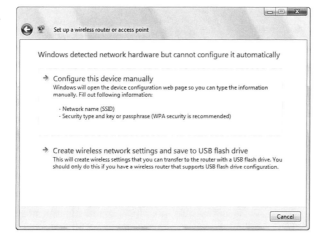

FIGURE 6.6

Entering a network name (SSID) for your network.

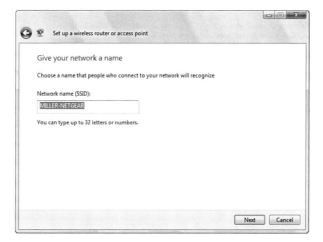

9. As shown in Figure 6.7, you're now prompted to create a passphrase for WPA wireless security. You can accept the nonsense passphrase that Windows generates for you, or you can enter something easier for you to remember. It must be at least 8 characters long.

FIGURE 6.7

Creating a passphrase for WPA wireless security.

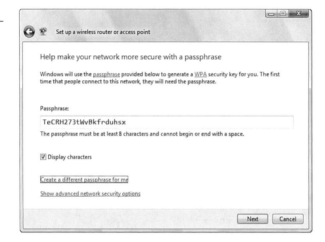

10. You're now prompted to configure the file and printer sharing options for your network. As you can see in Figure 6.8, you can choose to not allow file and printer sharing, allow password protected sharing, or allow sharing with anyone on your network. (Most users will choose this last option.)

FIGURE 6.8

Configuring file and printer sharing.

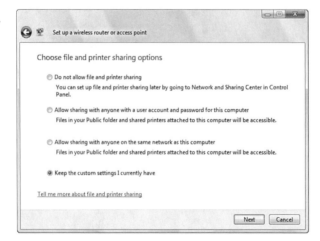

11. Finally, as shown in Figure 6.9, you're prompted to save your settings to a USB flash drive, which you can then use to copy your settings to computers on your network. Follow the onscreen instructions to do this.

FIGURE 6.9

Saving your configuration settings to a USB flash drive.

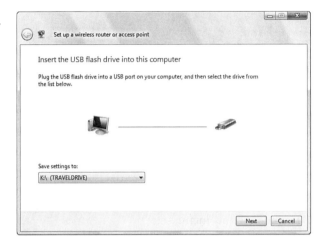

Connecting Other Windows Vista Computers to Your Network

Okay, you've just created your new network. By default, your main PC is automatically configured for and connected to the network. That leaves all the other computers you want to connect to the network to be configured.

To configure a computer for your network, you need to know some key network settings. These settings are then used to configure the additional computers. In particular, you need to know the network's SSID (network name) and any wireless security information—network security key, passphrase, and so forth.

The easiest way to configure your other computers is to save these network settings from your first PC to a USB flash drive, and then copy the settings from the flash drive to the additional PCs. When you used the Set Up a Wireless Router or Access Point Wizard, you should have been prompted to save your settings to a USB drive; assuming you did so, follow these steps to copy the settings to another PC:

1. Insert the USB flash drive into a USB port on the second computer.

2. When the AutoPlay dialog box appears, as shown in Figure 6.10, select Wireless Network Setup Wizard.

3. When the wizard launches, follow the onscreen instructions to apply the network settings to this computer.

FIGURE 6.10

Getting ready to configure a network computer with a USB flash drive.

If you don't have your network settings on a USB flash drive, you can manually configure this computer for network use. Follow these steps:

1. From the Windows Start menu, select Connect To.

2. When the list of wireless networks appears, as shown in Figure 6.11, select your wireless network and click Connect.

3. When prompted by the dialog box shown in Figure 6.12, enter the network security key or passphrase assigned on your main PC, and then click OK.

Network TIP

After you've connected and configured all your network computers, it's a good idea to test the network to make sure that all devices are really connected. On each PC, open the Start menu and select Network; when the Network Explorer opens, you should see icons for each computer connected to your network

FIGURE 6.11

Choose your wireless network from the list.

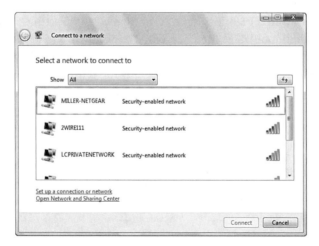

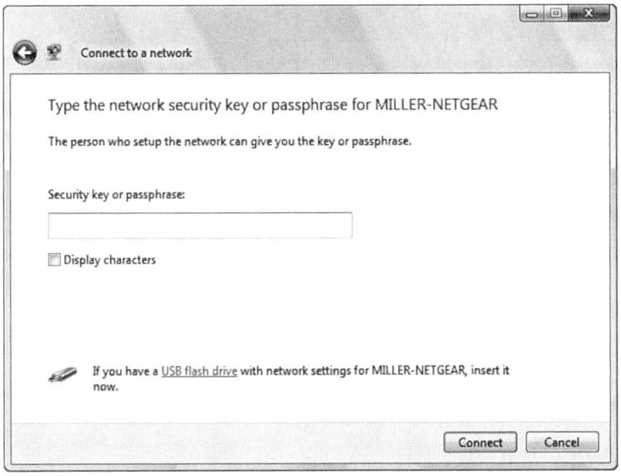

FIGURE 6.12

Enter your network security key or passphrase.

Connecting Windows XP Computers to Your Network

It's not necessary for all the computers on your network to be running Windows Vista; it's easy enough to mix and match PCs running Windows Vista, Windows XP, and other operating systems on the same network. That said, connecting a Windows XP computer to your network is slightly different from connecting Windows Vista computers.

Just as with a Vista computer, the easiest way to configure an XP computer is to use a USB flash drive to copy the network settings from the main PC. On a Windows XP computer, follow these steps:

1. Insert the USB flash drive into a USB port of the Windows XP computer.
2. When the AutoPlay dialog box appears, as shown in Figure 6.13, select Wireless Network Setup Wizard.
3. Follow the onscreen instructions to configure your computer using the settings found on the USB drive.

You can also manually add a Windows XP computer to your network, without use of a USB flash drive. Follow these steps:

1. Right-click the wireless network connection icon in the Windows system tray and select View Available Wireless Networks.
2. When the list of wireless networks appears, as shown in Figure 6.14, select your wireless network and then click Connect.
3. If you have security enabled for your wireless network, you'll be prompted to enter your network key or passphrase, as shown in Figure 6.15. Enter this key and then click Connect.

FIGURE 6.13

Use a USB flash drive to configure your Windows XP computer.

FIGURE 6.14

Selecting your wireless network in Windows XP.

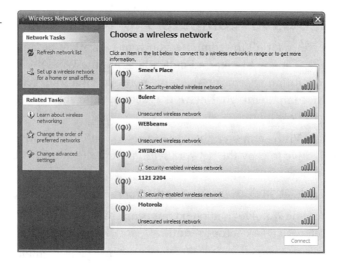

FIGURE 6.15

Entering your network key or passphrase in Windows XP.

That's it. Your Windows XP computer is now connected to your Windows Vista network.

Connecting a Windows Vista PC to an Older Wireless Network

Here's a possible scenario. You just purchased a new desktop or laptop PC with Windows Vista installed, and you want to connect that new computer to your existing wireless network. Your existing network, unfortunately, is not a Windows Vista network; the main computer on that network is running Windows XP or another older version of Windows. How do you configure this type of connection?

Fortunately, your Windows Vista PC doesn't care what type of network it's connected to. Nor does your network care what types of computers are connected to it. This makes it a relative snap to connect a newer computer to an older network.

First, of course, you have to make the connection between your new computer and the network. Assuming that you want to connect wirelessly, that probably means installing a wireless adapter on your new PC—unless it's a new notebook with built-in Wi-Fi. See Chapter 5 for detailed instructions.

After the wireless adapter is installed, you'll need to connect to and configure the network manually from this computer. You do this by opening the Windows Start menu and selecting Connect To. When the list of nearby wireless networks appears, select your wireless network and then click Connect. If you have security enabled for your wireless network, you'll be prompted to enter your network key or passphrase; do so and then click Connect. You're now connected to your existing network.

Network NOTE

The Connect To menu on the Windows Start menu is noticeably different in Windows Vista than in Windows XP. In Vista, you select Connect To to view all available wireless networks; in XP, you used this menu to view your technical network connections.

Managing Your Windows Vista Network

Just because your network is up and running doesn't mean you're finished with it. Windows Vista provides several ways to manage your network and its connected computers—which you may need to do if you ever want to change the initial configuration settings.

Getting to Know the Network and Sharing Center

In Windows Vista, all network management is accomplished from the new Network and Sharing Center. There are three ways to open this utility:

- Open the Start menu, select Network to open the Network Explorer, and then click the Network and Sharing Center button (as shown in Figure 6.16).

■ Open the Start menu, select Control Panel, select Network and Internet, and then click Network and Sharing Center (as shown in Figure 6.17).

■ Open the Start menu, enter **network** into the Search box, and then click Network and Sharing Center (as shown in Figure 6.18).

As you can see in Figure 6.19, the Network and Sharing Center displays a map of your current network, along with a variety of configuration settings. We'll discuss these settings next.

FIGURE 6.16

Click the Network and Sharing Center button in Network Explorer.

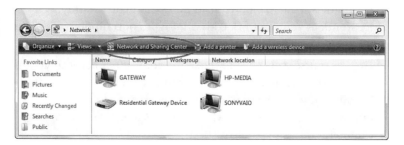

FIGURE 6.17

Click Network and Sharing Center in the Control Panel.

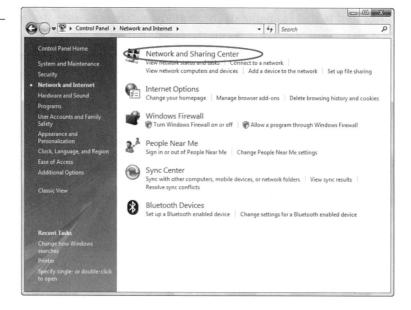

FIGURE 6.18

Searching for the
Network and
Sharing Center
from the Vista
Start menu.

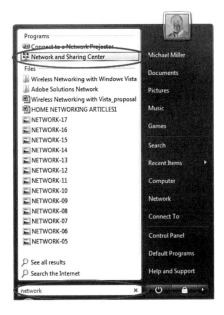

FIGURE 6.19

The focal point of
Vista network-
ing—the Network
and Sharing
Center.

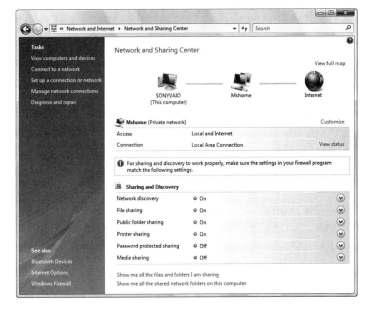

Changing Your Network Configuration

The Network and Sharing Center offers easy access to most key network configuration settings. These settings are located in the Sharing and Discovery part of the
window, in expandable sections, as shown in Figure 6.20; just click a section head-
ing to expand the section and see all configuration options.

FIGURE 6.20

Configuration settings in the Network and Sharing Center.

What can you configure from the Network and Sharing Center? Here's the list:

- Network discovery—Enables this computer to see other network computers, and vice versa.

- File sharing—Enables other users on your network to access shared files and printers on this computer.

- Public folder sharing—Lets other users on the network either view or view, edit, and create files stored in this computer's Public folder.

- Printer sharing—Lets other users on the network use printers connected to this computer.

- Password protected sharing—When enabled, limits access to public folders to those users who have an account and password on this computer.

- Media sharing—Enables users and devices on the network to access shared music, videos, and pictures stored on this computer. Also lets this computer access shared media files on other computers connected to the network.

Changing any of these settings is as simple as clicking the down arrow to expand a section, checking the desired setting(s), and then clicking the Apply button.

Viewing a Larger Network Map

The network map displayed in the Network and Sharing Center is a basic map that shows only the immediate connections for the current computer. To view a larger and more complete map of your entire network, click the View Full Map link in the Network and Sharing Center window.

As you can see in Figure 6.21, the Network Map window displays all your connected network devices. In this example, the main computer (SonyVaio) is connected to the switch within the wireless router, which then connects to the MillerNetwork router itself, which then connects to two wireless computers (HP-MEDIA and Gateway) and to the Internet. (The green bars next to each wireless PC indicates the signal strength to/from that PC.) To open any network computer or device, simply double-click its icon on the map.

FIGURE 6.21

Windows Vista's network map.

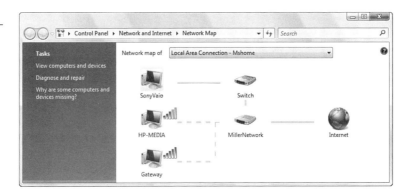

Changing Workgroups

All the computers in a network are part of what Microsoft calls a *workgroup*. Each workgroup has a name, and Windows automatically creates a workgroup for your computers when it first sets up a network.

That said, Windows lets you set up multiple workgroups on a network, lets you connect a computer to any available workgroup, and even lets you rename the existing workgroups.

Which workgroup you connect to is managed from Windows Vista's System Properties dialog box. Follow these steps to connect to a different workgroup:

1. From the Network and Sharing Center, expand the Network Discovery section and then click the Change Settings link next to the workgroup name, as shown in Figure 6.22.

2. When the System Properties dialog box appears, as shown in Figure 6.23, select the Computer Name tab and click the Change button.

Network CAUTION

Some Windows XP computers may not automatically appear in the network map, instead appearing by themselves below the map. That's because the map displays only those computers that have Link-Layer Topology Discovery (LLTD) installed. If you have a Windows XP computer that doesn't appear on the network map, you can download LLTD for that computer from support. microsoft.com/kb/922120.

FIGURE 6.22

Getting ready to edit your workgroup settings.

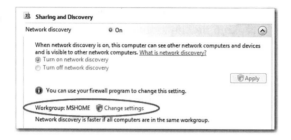

FIGURE 6.23

Viewing workgroup information in the System Properties dialog box.

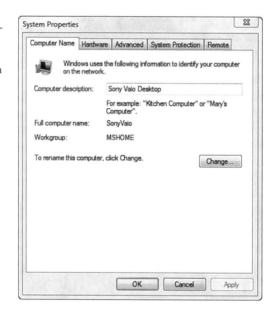

3. When the Computer Name Changes dialog box appears, as shown in Figure 6.24, go to the Workgroup field and enter the name of a different workgroup. (You can enter the name of an existing workgroup, or enter a new name to create a new workgroup.)

4. Click OK.

Changing the Type of Network Location

When you first connect your computer to the network, you are prompted to set your type of network location—Home, Work, or Public Place. You can later change the network location type for a given network connection by following these steps:

1. While logged on to the network, open the Network and Sharing Center and select Customize (next to your network name).

FIGURE 6.24

Changing your
computer's
workgroup.

2. When the Set Network Location window appears, as shown in Figure 6.25, select Public (for Public Place networks) or Private (for Home or Work networks).

3. Click the Next button and then click Close.

This window also lets you change the name of your network. Windows assigns a default name to your network, typically MSHOME or something similar. If you want your network to have a more descriptive moniker, open the Set Network Location window and enter a new name into the Network Name field.

Network CAUTION

You'll need to change the network name on all computers connected to your network, or your computers will think they're part of different networks.

FIGURE 6.25

Changing net-
work location
settings.

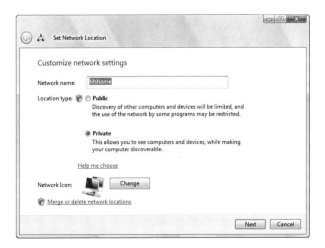

Managing Network Connections

To view information about your current network connection—connection speed, amount of data transmitted, and the like—as well as to manage the connection itself, you use the Network Connections folder. To access this folder, open the Network and Sharing Center and click Manage Network Connections (in the Tasks pane).

As you can see in Figure 6.26, the Network Connections folder displays icons for each available network connection on this PC. Depending on your computer and available networks, there may be an icon for both a wired and a wireless network— and, if you have a Bluetooth keyboard or mouse connected, for a Bluetooth network.

FIGURE 6.26

Managing
your network
connections.

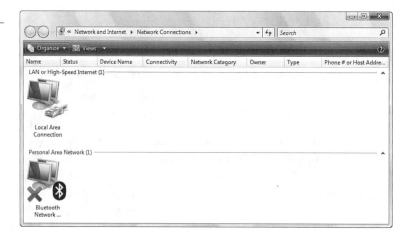

To view and manage a given connection, double-click the connection's icon. This opens the Status dialog box, like the one shown in Figure 6.27. From here you can:

- Click the Details button to view even more technical details about this connection, as shown in Figure 6.28.

- Click the Properties button to edit various technical properties for this connection, including the underlying TCP/IP protocols, as shown in Figure 6.29.

Network TIP

You can also open the Properties dialog box by right-clicking a connection in the Network Connections folder and selecting Properties from the pop-up window.

FIGURE 6.27

Viewing and editing information about a particular network connection.

FIGURE 6.28

Viewing more technical details about the connection.

■ Click the Diagnose button if you're having network problems and need to troubleshoot.

■ Click the Disable button to disable this particular connection.

Network TIP

To rename a network connection, right-click the connection's icon in the Network Connections folder and select Rename. The connection's name is now highlighted; type a new name and then press Enter on your computer keyboard.

FIGURE 6.29

Editing a connection's technical properties.

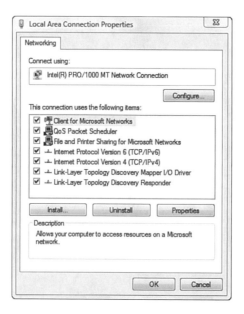

Changing IP Addresses

As you learned in Chapter 3, "How Windows Vista Handles Wireless Networking," Windows uses TCP/IP technology to enable network communication between multiple computers. By default, Windows uses the Dynamic Host Configuration Protocol (DHCP) to automatically assign each computer on your network its own unique Internet Protocol (IP) address; this means you don't have to bother with creating an address for each PC.

In some circumstances it may be necessary to assign one or more PCs on your network its own specific IP address. For example, some print servers require a specific address (or an address in a given range) for the host computer; without the specific address, the print server doesn't know which PC it's connected to.

In most instances when assigning a manual IP address is necessary, the manufacturer of the given device will indicate what address or range of addresses you should use. To manually assign a specific IP address to the current PC, follow these steps:

1. Open the Network Connections folder.

2. Right-click the connection you want to change and select Properties from the pop-up menu.

Network TIP

In some instances you may need to indicate specific DNS server address settings to establish an Internet connection. If your Internet service provider supplies you with this information, open the IPv4 or IPv6 dialog box, check Use the Following DNS Server Addresses, and then enter the desired addresses into the Primary DNS Server and Alternate DNS Server boxes.

3. When the Properties dialog box appears, select either Internet Protocol Version 4 or Internet Protocol Version 6; then click the Properties button.

4. If you selected IPv4, select Use the Following IP Address (shown in Figure 6.30) and enter the appropriate settings into the IP Address, Subnet Mask, and Default Gateway boxes.

5. If you selected IPv6, select Use the Following IPv6 Address (shown in Figure 6.31) and enter the appropriate settings into the IPv6 Address, Subnet Prefix Length, and Default Gateway boxes.

6. Click OK when finished.

FIGURE 6.30

Manually entering an IPv4 address.

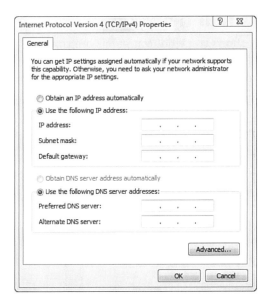

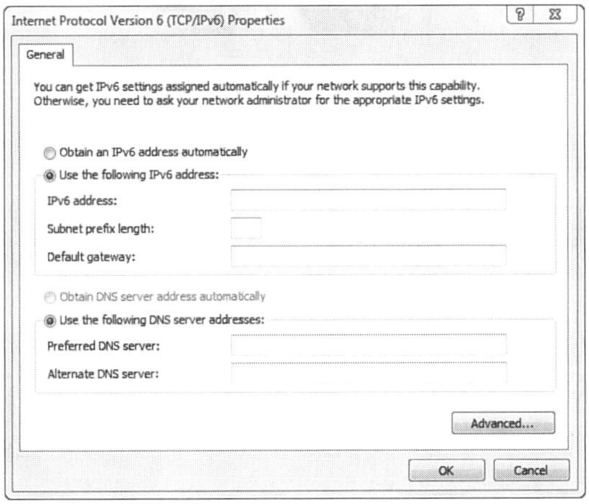

FIGURE 6.31

Manually entering an IPv6 address.

Disconnecting Your Computer from a Network

Windows makes it easy to disconnect from a network without physically disconnecting cables or devices. Just follow these steps:

1. Open the Network Connections folder.

2. To disconnect from a wireless network, right-click the icon for the current network and then select Disconnect.

3. To disconnect from an Ethernet network, right-click the icon for the current network and then select Disable.

Accessing Computers on Your Network

The network map only shows you what computers are connected to your network; it doesn't let you access the data stored on those computers. To access your network computers, you have to use the Network Explorer, where all network computers and resources are displayed.

Accessing Network Computers—And Shared Folders

You access the computers connected to your network from the Network Explorer folder, shown in Figure 6.32. To open this folder, open the Windows Start menu and select Network. That's all there is to it.

FIGURE 6.32

Access all networked computers from the Network Explorer.

As you can see, each computer connected to your network is displayed as an icon in the Network Explorer folder. To view the shared drives and folders for a given PC, just double-click the computer's icon. You can then navigate through all public folders and shared printers, as shown in Figure 6.33, as well as access or open individual files.

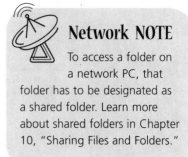

Network NOTE

To access a folder on a network PC, that folder has to be designated as a shared folder. Learn more about shared folders in Chapter 10, "Sharing Files and Folders."

FIGURE 6.33

Viewing the
shared contents
of a networked
computer.

In Windows XP, you access network computers and shared folders from the My
Network Places window, shown in Figure 6.34. You open this window by selecting
My Network Places from the Windows Start menu. Unlike Vista's Network Explorer,
My Network Places doesn't display networked computers; instead, it displays short-
cuts for all shared folders. To view the networked computers, select View Workgroup
Computers from the Network Tasks panel on the left side of the window.

FIGURE 6.34

Accessing net-
work resources in
Windows XP.

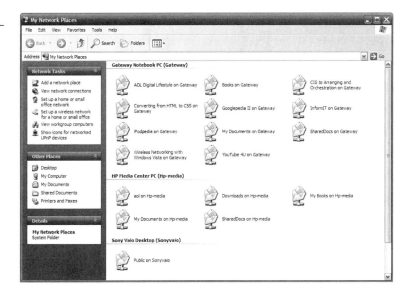

Creating a Shortcut to a Shared Folder

By default, only network computers are displayed in the Network Explorer folder. If you regularly access a particular shared folder on a given computer, you might find it easier to create a shortcut directly to that folder in the Network Explorer folder. Here's how to do it:

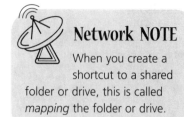

Network NOTE

When you create a shortcut to a shared folder or drive, this is called *mapping* the folder or drive.

1. From the computer that contains the shared folder, open the Windows Start menu and select Computer.

2. When the Computer Explorer opens, select the drive that contains the shared folder.

3. Press the Alt button your keyboard to display the Computer Explorer menu bar; then select Tools, Map Network Drive.

4. When the Map Network Drive window appears, as shown in Figure 6.35, select the desired drive from the Drive list.

FIGURE 6.35

Getting ready to map a shared folder.

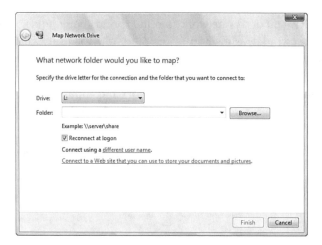

5. Click the Browse button to navigate to and select the desired shared folder, as shown in Figure 6.36; then click OK.

6. Click the Finish button.

FIGURE 6.36

Selecting the shared folder to map.

This creates an icon for the shared folder in the Network Explorer folder. All computers connected to the network will see this new shortcut icon and be able to directly access the shared folder by double-clicking the icon.

Next: Setting Up a Wireless Internet Connection

One popular use of a wireless network is to share an Internet connection between multiple computers. Learn how to configure your network to share an Internet connection in Chapter 7, "Setting Up—And Sharing—A Wireless Internet Connection," which follows next.

In this chapter

7

Setting Up—And Sharing— A Wireless Internet Connection

One of the primary reasons most home users install a wireless network is to share a common Internet connection between multiple computers. Fortunately, sharing an Internet connection is one of the easiest things to set up on a wireless network—assuming you have a fast enough Internet connection, that is.

Sharing an Internet Connection—Issues and Opportunities

As easy as sharing a wireless Internet connection is, there are some issues involved with the process. In particular, you need to determine whether your Internet connection is fast enough to share, as well as who you want to share your connection with.

Speed Matters: Broadband Versus Dial-Up

More and more Americans are connecting to the Internet via fast broadband connections. These connections are provided via digital cable, digital subscriber line (DSL), or digital satellite technology; which options you have available to you depend on the services offered in your specific location.

A broadband connection has two advantages over the older dial-up type of connection. First, broadband connections are always on; you don't have to manually connect and log on when you want to go online. Second, broadband connections are much faster than dial-up connections; dial-up connections top off at 56Kbps, whereas broadband connections typically offer between 1Mbps and 3Mbps download speeds—at least 20 times faster than dial-up.

For both these reasons, a broadband connection is better for network sharing than is a dial-up connection. If you try to share a dial-up connection, you'll need to dial into and log on to your Internet service provider (ISP) every time someone on the network wants to go online. At best this makes connecting inconvenient; at worst it may keep some network computers from connecting (if your main PC isn't connected or logged on, for example). And if you try to share a too-slow connection, there simply won't be enough bandwidth available for multiple PCs to comfortably share.

Although it's not impossible to share a dial-up connection (and we'll discuss how, in the "Connecting with Internet Connection Sharing" section of this chapter), it's not really recommended. If you want to share an Internet connection, get a fast, always-on broadband connection before you connect it to your network.

Security Matters: To Share or Not to Share?

Sharing an Internet connection over a wireless network involves broadcasting that connection over the airwaves. When you broadcast an Internet signal in this fashion, you can choose to make the connection public, so anyone can use it, or private, so that only computers connected to your network have access.

To create a public wireless Internet connection, all you have to do is disable wireless security on your network. With no password required to log on, anyone within Wi-Fi range can access your wireless signal and connect to the Internet over your connection. Conversely, to keep others from leeching your Internet connection, enable wireless security; unless your neighbors know your network security key or passphrase, they can't log on and connect.

The question of whether to share your Internet connection is both social and technical in nature. The social aspect comes from the notion held by some that the Internet should be freely available for as many people as possible. If you have an Internet connection, the thinking goes, you're morally obligated to share that connection with others. (Or, at least, you see no harm from such sharing.) This argument ignores the fact that you're paying $30 or so a month for that Internet connection, and anyone tapping into your connection is getting it for free; you're not getting compensated for sharing your connection. That said, perhaps you don't care that your neighbors across the street are using your connection to access the Internet. Maybe you're just being a good neighbor.

The technical aspect concerns security. If someone can tap into your unsecured Internet connection that also means that person can tap into your unsecured network. If that person can access your Internet connection, he can also access files stored on your network computers. That's not a good thing. If you choose to share your Internet connection in this fashion (by not enabling wireless security), you should at least disable file and folder sharing on your network, and perhaps enable password protection to access network files. Sharing your Internet connection doesn't mean you have to put your own valuable data at risk.

There's an additional risk involved in publicly sharing an Internet connection. What happens if one of your neighbors uses your Internet connection to perform an illegal or unethical activity, such as sending out a raft of spam messages or illegally downloading music files from a file-sharing site? Because your Internet connection was used, you may be liable for damages related to that activity—even though you yourself didn't participate. You're in fact an accessory to the crime; and, because there may be no way to determine whether your PC was involved in the activity (or not), you may be presumed guilty until proven innocent.

These are all good reasons *not* to share your Internet connection—which argues in favor of enabling wireless security to keep your connection private. On the flip side, you may want to keep your network open, in spite of these risks, if you often have visitors who need to access the Internet. Instead of constantly fiddling with network settings on your guests' computers (typically involving the entering of that long and difficult-to-remember network security key or passphrase), you may want to keep your network public instead. With a nonprotected network, any guest can easily connect to the Internet simply by making a connection to your network's wireless signal. It's the equivalent of establishing your own public Wi-Fi hot spot, just like the one in your local coffeehouse.

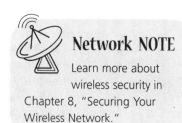

Network NOTE

Learn more about wireless security in Chapter 8, "Securing Your Wireless Network."

Networks Don't Matter: Broadcasting Internet to a Single Computer

Before we get to the nuts and bolts of setting up a shared Internet connection, there's one more issue to examine. I said previously that one of the most common reasons to set up a wireless network was to share an Internet connection between multiple computers. But you may want to set up a wireless Internet connection if you have just one PC in your house—particularly if that PC is a notebook model.

One of the nice things about having a notebook PC is that you're not tethered to using it in a single room. Thanks to the battery operation, you can pick up and carry your notebook PC to any room in your house—or even outdoors, if you like. But you can't do this if you need to connect to the Internet and your Internet connection is a physical one. (That is, if you have to connect your notebook via cable to your broadband modem.)

This is where a simple wireless network comes in. Connect your broadband modem to a wireless router and then connect your notebook PC wirelessly to the router. Your Internet connection is beamed wirelessly from the router to your PC, wherever it happens to be at the moment. So even though you're not sharing files with another computer, the capability to extend the Internet signal to any room in your house (or even outdoors) provides a degree of flexibility that you didn't have previously.

Different Ways to Share

There are three different ways to share an Internet connection on a wireless network. Which method you choose depends on your particular needs and, perhaps, the equipment available to you:

- The first method, using Windows' Internet Connection Sharing, is best if you want to share a dial-up connection. With this approach, your modem connects directly to the main PC in your network; the sharing of that connection is done through that PC.

- The second method, using a combination wireless router/modem, is sometimes an option if that particular piece of equipment is offered by your Internet service provider. The Internet line runs directly into the router/modem, which then beams the Internet signal (along with other network signals) to all the computers on your network. The advantage of this approach, of course, is that you only have one piece of equipment instead of two (separate router and modem). In addition, this device is often provided free (or at a reduced rate) by your cable or DSL company; in some instances, you may even get them to come out and install everything, which saves you that time and expense.

■ The third and most common method of sharing an Internet connection, however, involves a separate wireless router, which you provide and connect to your ISP's broadband modem. This type of setup is the most flexible (you can upgrade your router whenever you want without having to change the modem) and is relatively easy to configure.

Connecting Via a Wireless Router

The most common type of wireless Internet setup uses a separate wireless router and broadband modem, as shown in Figure 7.1.

Setting Up the Modem and Router

Fortunately, this type of setup isn't too difficult; just follow these steps:

FIGURE 7.1

A home network utilizing a separate broadband modem and wireless router.

Cable Outlet   Cable Modem   Wireless Router   Main PC

1. Connect a coaxial cable between the cable/DSL wall outlet and the broadband modem.

2. Connect an Ethernet cable between your broadband modem and your wireless router. (Most routers have a dedicated "modem in" connection, although you can connect the cable to any Ethernet port on your router.)

3. Connect an Ethernet cable between the wireless router and your main PC.

4. Configure the wireless router for network use, using the unit's accompanying installation software.

5. Set up your network from the main PC.

Configuring Your Computer for an Internet Connection

That last step in the previous section is only necessary if you're setting up an entire multiple-computer network. If you only want to share an Internet connection, with no other network functions, the setup is simpler. Follow these steps:

1. Open the Windows Start menu and select Control Panel.

2. From the Control Panel, select Network and Internet.

3. When the Network and Internet window appears, select Network and Sharing Center.

4. When the Network and Sharing Center opens, click Set Up a Connection or Network (in the Tasks pane).

5. When the Set Up a Connection or Network Wizard appears, as shown in Figure 7.2, select Connect to the Internet and then click Next.

6. This launches the Connect to the Internet Wizard, shown in Figure 7.3. Select which type of connection you have—Broadband or Dial-up.

7. If you have a broadband connection, enter your username, password, and connection name, as shown in Figure 7.4. Check the Allow Other People to Use This Connection option; then click Connect.

8. If you have a dial-up connection, select which modem you want to use; then enter your ISP's phone number, your username and password, and the connection name. Check the Allow Other People to Use This Connection option and then click Connect.

FIGURE 7.2

Getting ready to set up an Internet connection.

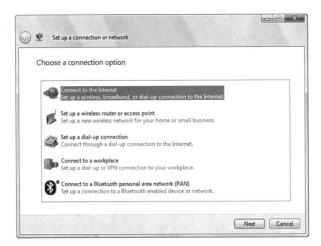

FIGURE 7.3

Selecting your particular type of connection.

FIGURE 7.4

Configuring a broadband connection.

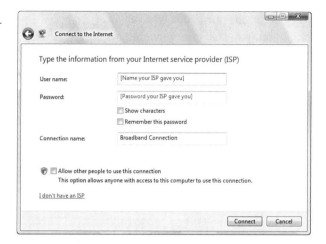

After you've set up everything, any computer connected to your wireless network should have automatic access to your Internet connection.

Connecting Via a Combination Router/Modem Gateway

If your cable or DSL company offers a combination router/modem gateway device, sharing an Internet connection gets even easier. This single piece of equipment serves as both your broadband modem and your wireless network router; connect your incoming Internet cable to this unit, and it both beams the Internet connection to all your wireless computers and manages all network data transfer and communications.

Figure 7.5 shows how a network using a router/modem gateway looks. The connection is relatively straightforward:

FIGURE 7.5

A home network utilizing a combination router/modem gateway.

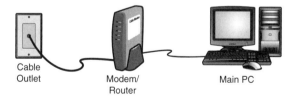

Cable Outlet   Modem/Router   Main PC

1. Connect a coaxial cable between your cable/DSL wall outlet and the router/modem.

2. Connect an Ethernet cable between the router/modem and your main PC.

3. Configure the router/modem for network use, using the unit's accompanying installation software.

4. Set up your network from the main PC.

That's the advantage of this particular type of setup—it's easy. In fact, your ISP may provide low- or no-cost setup services; check to see what's available with your particular service plan.

Connecting with Internet Connection Sharing

If you have a dial-up Internet connection, that connection has to be made through a single computer connected to your dial-up modem. In fact, in many instances, the dial-up modem is actually contained within the computer. You then use this host computer to dial in to your ISP and connect to the Internet.

To share this type of Internet connection, the other computers on your network have to first connect to the host PC and go through that PC to the Internet. (Figure 7.6 shows how this looks.) This is accomplished by an older Windows technology called Internet Connection Sharing (ICS). ICS is built into both Windows Vista and Windows XP.

Network NOTE

Most dial-up modems cannot be directly connected to a network router; the modem has to first connect to a host PC, which then connects to the router to share the connection via Internet Connection Sharing.

Network CAUTION

You should only use ICS if you want to share a dial-up connection—which may be too slow to share, anyway. You do not use ICS to share a broadband connection. (Although you can if you want to....)

FIGURE 7.6

A home network utilizing Internet Connection Sharing to connect to the Internet.

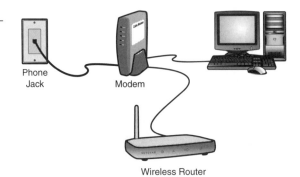

Phone Jack

Modem

Wireless Router

Setting Up an ICS Network

The first step in setting up ICS is to physically connect your modem, host computer, and wireless router. Here's how it all goes:

1. Connect a standard telephone cable between the nearest phone jack and the "phone in" jack on your dial-up modem. (If your modem is built into your PC, connect to the cable to the "phone in" jack on the back of your PC.) Connect your modem to a power source.

2. If you have an external modem, connect it (typically via USB) to your host PC. Connect it to a power source.

3. Connect an Ethernet cable between your host PC and your wireless router.

4. Power up and configure each piece of equipment.

Configuring Your Host PC for ICS

After your modem, host computer, and wireless router are physically connected in this fashion, you then have to configure your host computer for ICS. This is not an easy process.

Follow these steps:

1. Open the Windows Start menu and select Control Panel.

2. When the Control Panel opens, select Network and Internet.

3. When the Network and Internet window appears, select Network and Sharing Center.

4. From the Network and Sharing Center, click Manage Network Connections.

5. When the Network Connections window appears, right-click the connection you want to share and then select Properties.

6. When the Properties dialog box appears, select the Sharing tab. (The Sharing tab is only available if you have two network connections on this computer— one for the Internet connection to your modem, and a second to your network router.)

7. Select the option to Allow Other Network Users to Connect Through This Computer's Internet Connection.

8. Click OK.

Configuring IP Addresses for ICS

You're not finished yet. When you enable ICS on your host computer, your network is configured with a static IP address. Because this isn't the way you want things configured (to connect to the Internet, each PC on your network needs a dynamically assigned IP address), you'll need to reconfigure the TCP/IP settings for the host computer. Follow these steps:

1. Open the Network and Sharing Center and click Manage Network Connections (in the Tasks pane).

2. When the Network Connections window appears, right-click the LAN connection and then select Properties.

3. When the Properties dialog box appears, select either Internet Protocol Version 4 or Internet Protocol Version 6; then click Properties.

4. When the next Properties dialog box appears, select either Obtain an IP Address Automatically or Obtain an IPv6 Address Automatically.

5. Click OK when finished.

Configuring Your Other PCs for ICS

There's still more work to do. (I told you this wasn't an easy process!) All the computers on your network that want to share your dial-up Internet connection also have to be configured for ICS. Follow these steps for all the other computers on your network (but not the host):

1. Open the Windows Start menu and select Control Panel.

2. From the Control Panel, select Network and Internet.

3. When the Network and Internet window appears, select Internet Options.

4. When the Internet Properties dialog box appears, select the Connections tab.

5. Select the Never Dial a Connection option.

6. Click the LAN Settings button.

7. When the LAN Settings dialog box appears, uncheck the Automatically Detect Settings, Use Automatic Configuration Script, and Use a Proxy Server for Your LAN options.

8. Click OK.

After these configurations are made, you can connect to your ISP from your host computer, and then access this Internet connection from any other computer connected to your network.

Sharing Your Internet Connection with Others: Creating Your Own Public Wi-Fi Hot Spot

As discussed previously in this chapter, you can—if you want—configure your network so that any wireless computer in range can freely access your Internet connection. This effectively turns your network into a public Wi-Fi hot spot.

In fact, the process of publicly sharing an Internet connection is identical to that of setting up a Wi-Fi hot spot. A *hot spot*, after all, is just a wireless network with no wireless security set up; because you don't have to enter a network key or passphrase, any wireless computer can access the network and thus the Internet connection.

Configuring Your Wireless Router for Public Internet Access

You don't need any special equipment to set up a public wireless Internet connection; a standard wireless router and broadband modem will do the job. Here's how you make your shared Internet connection public:

1. Set up your broadband modem and wireless router as normal.

2. When prompted to enable wireless security, choose not to.

That's that. Without wireless security enabled, your network and Internet connection are now completely public.

Network CAUTION

If you choose to share your Internet connection publicly, you should enable password protection and disable file sharing for your network to protect your private data files. See Chapter 8 for more detailed instructions.

Setting Up a Wi-Fi Hot Spot with a Wireless Access Point

That said, if you're creating a public Wi-Fi hot spot for commercial use—that is, with no need for typical networking functions—you don't need or particularly want a fully featured wireless router. Instead, a better choice might be a single-function wireless access point, such as the one shown in Figure 7.7. A wireless access point of this type is kind of like a wireless router without the network router functions.

FIGURE 7.7

D-Link's DWL-2100AP AirPlus XtremeG Wireless Access Point—for residential or commercial use.

The advantage of using a wireless access point instead of a wireless router is simplicity. It's pretty much a plug and play affair; connect an Ethernet cable between your broadband modem and the access point, power everything up, and you're good to go. There are configuration settings to tweak if you want to, but they're seldom necessary—unless you're using the device for commercial use. (When you're running a public Wi-Fi hot spot, you want some control over how the access point is used.)

It's that capability to handle commercial usage that makes a typical wireless access point more expensive than a similar wireless router. Expect to pay anywhere from $80 to $300 for a wireless access point; the higher-priced models are better suited for day-in, day-out commercial use.

Next: Securing Your Wireless Network

Throughout this chapter we've touched on the need to secure your wireless network against unauthorized access—especially if you're publicly sharing your Internet connection. Network security is extremely important, so turn the page to learn all about it in Chapter 8, "Securing Your Wireless Network."

Network NOTE

As you recall from Chapter 4, "Designing Your Wireless Network—And Choosing Network Equipment," a wireless router is a single unit that combines network router and wireless access point functions.

Network NOTE

Wireless access points aren't limited to Wi-Fi hot spot use. Many large businesses use wireless access points to provide wireless access to their Ethernet-based corporate networks.

In this chapter

8

Securing Your Wireless Network

Any time you connect two or more computers together (and that includes connecting your computer to another computer on the Internet) you run the risk of unauthorized access. That is, it's possible that your computer can be accessed by someone who shouldn't be accessing it. And when unauthorized access occurs, bad things happen.

The only surefire way to keep the data and programs on a given computer safe from unauthorized users is to never connect that computer to a network—or to the Internet. Of course, if you've already set up your wireless network or Internet connection, the horse is already out of the barn, so to speak. What you need to do now is protect that computer from potential harm from that open door.

What we're talking about is wireless security—a catch-all term for various ways to protect your home or small business network from unwanted intrusion or attack.

Facing the Dangers of Wireless Networking

One of the issues with a wireless network is that all your data is just out there, broadcast over the air via radio waves, for anyone to grab. You see, when you connect your computer to a network or to the Internet, not only can your PC access other computers, but other computers can also access *your* PC. Unless you take precautions, malicious hackers (other network users or individuals on the Internet) can access your PC and steal important data, delete files and folders, or use your computer (via remote control) to attack other computers. The risk of outside attack is even more pronounced if you have an always-on Internet connection, such as that offered with DSL and cable broadband.

Different Types of Intrusions

There are many different ways that your PC can be attacked. These different types of attacks—more accurately called *intrusions*—include the following:

- Data theft—In this type of intrusion, the attacker steals valuable data stored on your computer—usernames, passwords, credit card numbers, bank account numbers, and so on. This can lead to the crime known as *identity theft*, where the person who stole your data uses that information to impersonate you online, using your personal and financial data to steal money from your bank account, using your credit card to make large purchases, and even using your Social Security number to establish a false identity.

- Data destruction—This type of intrusion is very damaging, because after the attacker gains access to your computer, he starts deleting things. The attacker deletes data files, program files, even the system files necessary to keep your computer up and running.

- Denial of service—This attack is designed to crash your system, typically by inundating it with hundreds and thousands of emails and other forms of electronic requests from other computers on the Internet. As your system receives more and more of these requests, it begins to slow down and then to crawl to a halt.

- Hijacking—Many attackers don't want to do harm to your PC, but rather to use your PC to do harm to other computer systems or websites. In a hijacking attack, the attacker surreptitiously installs backdoor software on your PC, so that he can operate it via remote control. With your PC under his control, the attacker then uses it—and thousands of other "zombie" computers—to initiate a larger denial of service attack on another system.

- Signal leeching—This type of intrusion isn't an attack per se, but rather a theft of services—in particular, your Internet connection. If your wireless network is configured for public access, with no security key or password required, anyone with a wireless PC in range of your wireless router can tap into your network and your wireless Internet connection. Although this type of intrusion causes no immediate harm to your computer or network, it does steal part of your Internet bandwidth—which you're paying for.

How to Tell If Your Computer Has Been Attacked

What are the signs that your computer is under attack, or being used to attack another computer? Here are some behaviors to look out for:

- An unusual amount of hard disk activity—especially when your PC isn't being used.
- An unusual amount of Internet access—especially when you're not browsing the Web or using email.
- An unusual number of email messages appearing in your inbox.
- Your Internet connection appears to slow down, taking longer to load web pages and download files.
- Missing or edited files on your hard disk.
- Unusual behavior—lots of pop-up windows, programs launching of their own accord, sluggish performance, and the like.

How to Protect Your PC from Intrusion

If the threat of unwanted intrusion scares you, that's good—you should be scared. Fortunately, you can take a number of steps to reduce your risk of attack and to minimize the impact if an intrusion does occur.

The key to protecting a network is to create as many obstacles as possible for a potential cracker. Although no network can be 100% secure, the more effort an attacker has to make, the more likely he'll give up and try a network that's easier to break into.

So how can you protect against unauthorized access to your wireless network? By using a little common sense, along with enabling basic security procedures, including the following:

- Activate the wireless security technology built into your Wi-Fi router. This wireless security, in the form of encrypted or password access, should keep all but the most dedicated hackers from accessing your wireless network.
- Change the default password for your wireless router. (You'd be surprised how many wireless networks can be accessed by entering the default "PASSWORD" password.)

■ Change the default network name (also called a *service set identifier*, or *SSID*) of your wireless access router.

■ Disable broadcast SSID function on your wireless router (if possible), so that the name of your network isn't publicly broadcast to the world at large.

■ Physically locate your wireless router toward the center of your home or office—not near the windows, where it can extend the range of your network well outside your building.

Network TIP

Windows Vista includes an easy-to-use backup utility. To access Vista's Backup and Restore center, open the Start menu and select All Programs, Accessories, System Tools, Backup Status and Configuration.

■ Install and activate a firewall program on every PC on your home network to block attacks from outside your network.

■ Install and regularly update antivirus and antispyware utilities on each PC on your network.

■ Deactivate file sharing on your PCs, so attackers won't be able to access your personal files.

■ Make regular backup copies of your important data—just in case.

We'll discuss most of these steps throughout this chapter.

New Security Features in Windows Vista

The Microsoft Windows operating system has long been a particular target of computer attackers, simply because so many people use it. Hackers go after big targets, and the universe of Windows-based computers is vast.

That said, Microsoft has made great strides in improving the security of its operating system. This is particularly noticeable in Windows Vista, which sports numerous security improvements over previous versions of Windows.

What's new in Windows Vista, security-wise? Here's a short list:

■ User Account Control (UAC)—Prevents unauthorized people and processes from taking control of your system and installing and running malicious programs

■ Windows Firewall—Improved to better protect your system from outside attack

■ Windows Service Hardening—Limits the access privileges of system services, thus guarding against viruses and spyware that can take control of key Windows processes

- Protected Mode for Internet Explorer—Isolates suspicious programs in their own private "sandbox"
- Microsoft Phishing filter—Protects against fraudulent emails and websites
- Windows Defender—Guards against malicious spyware

Microsoft's goal with all these technologies is to make your system more secure, without requiring undue effort on your part. Certainly, a Windows Vista PC is more secure than a Windows XP computer.

Enabling Wireless Security

Network CAUTION

Without some form of wireless security, anyone with a wireless PC can tap into your wireless network. At the very least, they can steal bandwidth from your Internet connection. Worst case, they might be able to access the personal files stored on your PC.

Securing a wireless network is more challenging than securing a wired network. When you're transmitting network signals via radio waves, anyone within range can receive your signals. You need to secure those signals to keep outsiders from listening or breaking in to your network.

To keep outsiders from tapping into your wireless network, you can assign to your network a fairly complex encryption code, called a *network key*, via your wireless router's configuration settings. To access your network, a computer must know the code—which, unless it's officially part of your network, it won't.

There are several ways to assign a network key to your network. Most wireless routers come with configuration utilities that let you easily activate this type of wireless security, typically during the router's installation/setup process. In addition, you can use Windows' built-in wireless security function, which adds the same encryption via the operating system.

Different Types of Wireless Security

Four primary types of wireless security are in use today. All these security protocols require the use of a network key. This network key may be generated automatically by your network router or adapter, or you may have to specify the key by typing it yourself. The longer the network key, the greater the encryption—and the more secure your wireless network will be.

The four types of wireless security include the following, with the most secure listed first:

- WPA2—WPA stands for Wi-Fi Protected Access, and the new WPA2 standard offers the strongest level of security available today. With WPA2 (and the

older WPA standard), network keys are
automatically changed on a regular basis.

- WPA—This is the older, slightly less secure
version of Wi-Fi Protected Access security,
still a good choice for securing most small
networks.

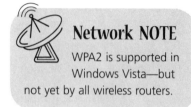

Network NOTE

WPA2 is supported in
Windows Vista—but
not yet by all wireless routers.

- WEP 128-bit—*WEP* stands for *Wired Equivalent
Privacy*. There are two levels of WEP protection, the stronger 128-bit and the
weaker 64-bit.

- WEP 64-bit—This is the weakest level of wireless protection available. If you
have an older laptop PC or wireless adapter, you may have to use this level
of protection instead of WEP 128-bit or WPA/WPA2.

You should choose the highest level of protection supported by all the equipment on
your network—your wireless router, wireless adapters, and notebook PCs. If just one
piece of equipment doesn't support a higher level of security, you have to switch to
the next-highest level; the security level you choose has to fit the lowest common
denominator, as defined by the wireless equipment in use.

So if your wireless router and all your wireless adapters and notebook PCs support
WPA or WPA2 encryption, you should switch to that method because it provides the
strongest protection. Otherwise, choose either WEP 128-bit (preferred) or WEP 64-bit
encryption.

Configuring Your Network for Wireless Security

To set the wireless security for your network and assign network keys, you can use
the setup utility that came with your wireless router. Alternately, you can configure
Windows to manually assign network keys to each computer on your network.

Wireless Security in Windows Vista

In Windows Vista, you enable wireless security via the Set Up a Wireless Router or
Access Point Wizard. To get to the wizard, open the Control Panel and select
Network and Internet, Network and Sharing Center, and then Set Up a Connection
or Network. In the next window, select Set Up a Wireless Router or Access Point. This
launches the wizard.

Click the Next button until Windows automatically detects your network hardware
and settings. From here you can give your network an SSID name (different from
the name assigned in the Network Setup Wizard), and then either automatically
assign or manually enter a network key or passphrase, as shown in Figure 8.1. The
type and length of the key you choose depends on the type of encryption you
choose, of course.

FIGURE 8.1

Assigning a network key in Windows Vista.

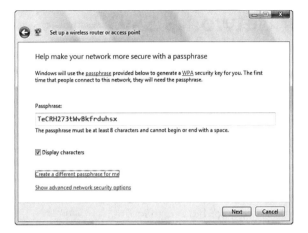

After the key is assigned, write it down. That's because you'll need to run this wizard on all the other PCs on the network and manually enter this same key for each computer. (Alternately, Windows lets you save the key to a USB drive, which you can then transfer to your other PCs.) After all the work is done, only those PCs that have been assigned this specific key can connect to your wireless network—which means no more neighbors leeching off your wireless connection.

Wireless Security in Windows XP

In Windows XP, you configure wireless security via the Wireless Network Setup Wizard. To run the wizard, open the Control Panel and click the Wireless Network Setup Wizard icon.

After you launch the wizard, you proceed just as you do with the similar wizard in Windows Vista. As you can see in Figure 8.2, you choose an SSID name and then set your network key. As with the Vista wizard, make sure you write down the key, as you'll need it to activate the wireless security on the other PCs on your network.

FIGURE 8.2

Assigning a network key in Windows XP.

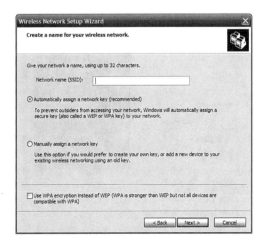

Protecting Your Network's SSID

Every wireless network has a name, otherwise known as its SSID (Service Set Identifier). The SSID is assigned by your wireless router.

Changing the SSID and Password

Many router companies use their company names as the default SSID. For example, a Linksys router might have an SSID labeled "LINKSYS." This type of common SSID could give your network the same name as other wireless networks in your neighborhood, which makes it easy for hackers to locate and gain access to your network.

Network NOTE

Sometimes the router adds a unique number to this name, such as "LINKSYS123." This type of unique numbering is more secure than generic naming but still is easily hacked.

For this reason, you should override your router's default SSID and assign a more unique name to your wireless network. It's going to be tougher for a hacker to guess that your network is named "MIKE_NETWORK_1007" than if it was generically named "LINKSYS."

You should be able to change the SSID from your router's configuration utility. (Figure 8.3 shows the configuration utility for a Netgear router; you change the SSID from the Wireless Settings page.)

FIGURE 8.3

Changing the SSID for a Netgear router.

Along the same lines, you should also change the default password for your router. Most routers come from the factory with a simple password assigned; often, the password is "PASSWORD." As you might suspect, it's relatively easy for a hacker to access a network if the default password is still in use. So when you go to change the router's SSID, change the password, too. (And the longer and more complex the password you create, the more difficult it will be to hack.)

Network CAUTION

If you change your SSID after you've set up other computers on your network, you'll need to reconfigure them to find and use the new SSID.

Disabling SSID Broadcasting

Most wireless routers, by default, constantly broadcast the network's SSID, so that all nearby computers will know that the network is there and ready to be connected to. The downside of this is that when an SSID is broadcast, anyone with a laptop PC or wireless access point receives notice of your network's name—which makes your network a more obvious target for hackers.

For this reason, you should configure your router to disable SSID broadcasting. If the SSID is not broadcast, your wireless network will be less visible to outsiders. When a hacker doesn't immediately see your network on his list of nearby wireless networks, he'll likely find another network to tap into.

Network CAUTION

When you disable SSID broadcasting, your own wireless computers won't be able to see your network either. This means you'll have to enter the SSID manually when you go to connect; see Chapter 14, "Connecting to Wi-Fi Hot Spots and Public Networks," for more information.

As with changing the SSID, you should be able to turn off SSID broadcasting from your router's configuration utility.

Installing and Configuring a Software Firewall

What happens if an intruder gets past your network key protection? Worst case scenario, an Internet-based hacker can tap into your network and access your individual computers, causing all manner of damage and even using your PCs as "zombies" for further attacks on other systems.

The best way to protect your system against outside attack is to block the path of attack with a *firewall*. A firewall is a software program that forms a virtual barrier between your computer and the Internet. The firewall selectively filters the data that is passed between both ends of the connection and protects your system against outside attack.

Using the Windows Firewall

If you're running Windows Vista or Windows XP, you already have a firewall program installed on your system. The Windows Firewall is activated by default, although you can always check to make sure that it's up and working properly. In Windows Vista, open the Control Panel and select Security, Windows Firewall. When the Windows Firewall window appears, as shown in Figure 8.4, you can turn the firewall on and off, choose to allow particular programs through the firewall, or click Change Settings to configure the firewall's settings.

FIGURE 8.4

Checking the Windows Firewall settings in Windows Vista.

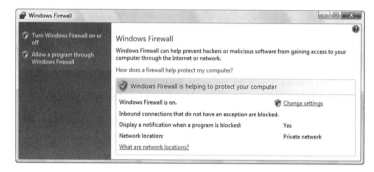

In Windows XP, open the Control Panel and go to the Windows Security Center. All of Windows security settings are visible there, including those for the Windows Firewall.

Using Third-Party Firewall Software

For most users, the Windows Firewall is more than enough protection against computer attacks. That said, there are also a number of third-party firewall programs available, most of which are more robust and offer more protection than Windows' built-in firewall. The best of these programs include

- AOL Firewall (free, daol.aol.com/safetycenter/firewall/)
- BlackICE PC Protection ($39.95-$49.95 with discounts for multiple computers, blackice.iss.net)
- Free ZoneAlarm (free, www.zonealarm.com)
- Norton Personal Firewall ($49.99, www.symantec.com)
- PC Tools Firewall Plus (free, www.pctools.com/firewall/)
- Sunbelt Personal Firewall ($19.95, www.sunbelt-software.com/Home-Home-Office/Sunbelt-Personal-Firewall/)
- ZoneAlarm Pro ($39.95, www.zonealarm.com)

Protecting Against Viruses and Spyware

A *computer virus* is a malicious software program designed to do damage to your computer system by deleting files or even taking over your PC to launch attacks on other systems. A virus attacks your computer when you run an infected software program, launching a "payload" that often is catastrophic. You obviously want to avoid virus infection—and cleanse the virus from your system if it happens to become infected.

Similar to but slightly different from computer viruses is a type of program called *spyware*, which installs itself on your computer and then surreptitiously sends information about the way you use your PC to some interested third party. Although spyware is not technically a computer virus, having spyware infect your system is almost as bad as being infected with a virus. Some spyware programs will even hijack your computer and launch pop-up windows and advertisements when you visit certain web pages. If there's spyware on your computer, you definitely want to get rid of it.

Network NOTE

Spyware typically gets installed in the background when you're installing another program. One of the biggest sources of spyware are peer-to-peer music-trading networks (*not* legitimate online music stores, such as the iTunes Store); when you install the file-trading software, the spyware is also installed.

Practicing Safe Computing

How do you protect your system against computer viruses and spyware? The only surefire way to avoid infection is to disconnect each individual computer from your network and from the Internet, and never insert any shared media (CDs, USB memory drives, floppy disks, and so on) into your system. That's right—the only guaranteed prevention is total isolation.

Because you're not going to completely isolate your computer from the outside world, you'll never be 100% safe from the threat of computer viruses. There are, however, some steps you can take to reduce your risk:

- Don't open email attachments from people you don't know—or even from people you *do* know, if you aren't expecting them. Most viruses today are transmitted via infected email attachments—and some viruses can hijack the address book on an infected PC, thus sending out infected email that the owner isn't even aware of.

- Don't accept any files sent to you via instant messaging.

- Download files only from reliable file archive websites, such as Download.com (www.download.com) and Tucows (www.tucows.com), not from anonymous downloading or peer-to-peer file sharing sites.

- Don't visit peer-to-peer file sharing sites, and don't install file sharing software.
- Don't execute programs you find in Usenet newsgroups or posted to web message boards or blogs.
- Don't click links sent to you from strangers via instant messaging or in a chat room.
- Don't click links that appear in unexpected pop-up windows.
- Share disks and files only with users you know and trust.
- Use antivirus software.

These precautions—especially the first one about not opening email attachments—should provide good insurance against the threat of computer viruses.

Using Antivirus Software

One of the primary lines of defense against virus infection is to install an antivirus software program on each PC in your network. Antivirus programs are capable of detecting known viruses and protecting your system against new, unknown viruses. These programs check your system for viruses each time your system is booted and can be configured to check any programs you download from the Internet. They're also used to disinfect your system if it becomes infected with a virus.

The most popular antivirus programs include

- AVG Anti-Virus Free Edition (free, www.grisoft.com)
- AVG Anti-Virus Professional Edition ($29.95, www.grisoft.com)
- Kaspersky Anti-Virus ($49.95-$59.95, www.kaspersky.com)
- McAfee VirusScan Plus ($39.99, www.mcafee.com)
- Norton AntiVirus ($39.99, www.symantec.com)
- Trend Micro AntiVirus plus AntiSpyware ($39.95, www.trendmicro.com)

Network NOTE
Pricing for most antivirus software is actually for a one-year subscription. You'll end up paying this figure every year to keep the software and its virus definitions up to date.

Network CAUTION
All of these antivirus programs do a good job—sometimes *too* good. I have personally had problems with Norton and McAfee antivirus products being too aggressive in protecting my system, resulting in system slow-downs and numerous program crashes. If you find your computer slowing down or freezing up after installing an antivirus program, you may need to uninstall that program and try another.

- Windows Live OneCare ($49.95 for 3 PCs, www.windowsonecare.com)
- ZoneAlarm Antivirus ($29.95, www.zonealarm.com)

My personal favorite antivirus program is Microsoft's Windows Live OneCare (shown in Figure 8.5), which is available for both Windows XP and Windows Vista. The $49.95 price lets you use the program on up to three different PCs, which makes it a real bargain for multiple-PC households and small offices. Windows Live OneCare also offers more than just antivirus protection; it also includes antispyware, antiphishing, firewall, and backup features.

FIGURE 8.5

Windows Live OneCare—an affordable antivirus program for both Windows Vista and Windows XP.

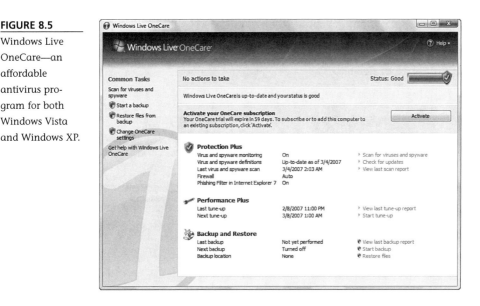

I'm also a big fan of the AVG Anti-Virus Free Edition, mainly because it's free. You don't get socked for a yearly subscription fee, as you do with other programs, which makes it the program of choice for frugal users. (It also works pretty well and doesn't put an undue strain on your computer's system resources.)

Whichever antivirus program you choose, you'll need to go online periodically to update the virus definition database the program uses to look for known virus files. As new viruses are created every week, this file of known viruses must be updated accordingly. Remember this: Your antivirus software is next to useless if you don't keep it updated. An outdated antivirus program won't be capable of recognizing—and protecting against—the latest computer viruses.

Network CAUTION

If you're installing an antivirus program on a Windows Vista PC, make sure the program is designed to work with Windows Vista. (Not all antivirus programs are Vista-compatible.)

Using Antispyware Software

Unfortunately, most antivirus programs won't catch spyware because spyware isn't a virus. To track down and uninstall these programs, then, you need to run an antispyware utility. Fortunately, one of the best antispyware programs is free—and included as part of Windows Vista.

Network TIP

To download a free version of Windows Defender for Windows XP, go to www.microsoft.com/athome/security/spyware/software/.

That's right, Windows Vista includes the well-regarded Windows Defender antispyware utility. Windows Defender, shown in Figure 8.6, works by automatically scanning your computer on a periodic basis, comparing the programs installed on your PC with Microsoft's database of spyware programs. If a matching program is found, it is quarantined or deleted.

FIGURE 8.6

Finding hidden spyware programs with Windows Defender.

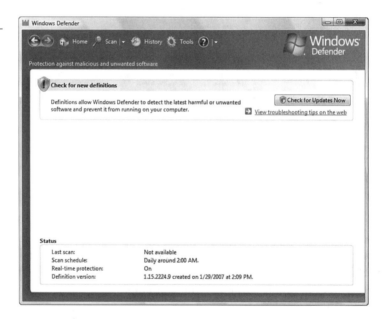

You access Windows Defender from the Windows Start menu. You can configure the program to scan your system at a designated time, or run an immediate scan. Defender also lets you configure the program to block or approve the running of designated programs, and includes the Software Explorer utility that lets you monitor and manage all programs that automatically load when Windows starts up. (Click the Tools button to access these added features, shown in Figure 8.7.)

FIGURE 8.7

The extra tools included with Windows Defender.

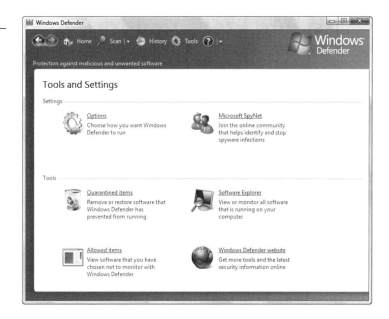

If you're interested in additional protection, you can choose from several other anti-spyware programs:

- Ad-Aware SE Personal (free, www.lavasoftusa.com)
- Ad-Aware SE Professional ($39.95, www.lavasoftusa.com)
- AVG Anti-Spyware ($29.95, www.grisoft.com)
- Spybot Search & Destroy (free, www.safer-networking.org)
- Trend Micro AntiSpyware ($29.95, www.trendmicro.com)
- Webroot Spy Sweeper ($29.95, www.webroot.com)
- ZoneAlarm Anti-Spyware ($29.95, www.zonealarm.com)

Network TIP

Some of the major Internet security suites, such as Norton Internet Security and the McAfee Internet Security Suite, include antispyware modules. Check the program's feature list before you buy.

Although Windows Defenders does a good job, it doesn't always catch all the spyware that's out there; in fact, no single spyware program can catch everything. (There's just too much spyware floating around!) For that reason, I occasionally like to supplement Windows Defender by running either Ad-Aware SE Personal or Spybot Search & Destroy. They're both free programs, and often catch spyware that Windows Defenders misses. (And vice versa, of course.)

Enabling Password Protection for File Sharing

One of the key reasons to set up a network is to let multiple users share your folders and files. However, you might not want *everyone* on your network to access your files; you certainly don't want intruders to have unfettered file access.

Windows Vista addresses this issue by introducing password-protected file sharing. When you choose to share folders and files over a network, you can also choose what level of access to allow:

- Public—Everyone on your network can access your Public folder and other folders you've designated for sharing.

- Password protected—Only users registered on the current computer can access shared folders.

With password protected access, only people with a user account and password for a specific computer can access the Public folder (and other shared folders) for that computer over the network. If a user doesn't have a user account and password, he can't access any folders on that computer.

To enable password protection, open the Windows Vista Network and Sharing Center and scroll down to the Sharing and Discovery section, shown in Figure 8.8. Click the down arrow next to Password Protected Sharing; then select Turn On Password Protected Sharing. Click the Apply button to finalize this configuration.

FIGURE 8.8

Enabling password protected file access in Windows Vista.

Of course, for password protected sharing to work, the same person must have an account on more than one computer—and be signed on to the second computer to access his files on the first. For example, if a user named Bob configures his main computer for password protected sharing, he must create a similar account named "Bob" on the second computer. Then, when he's logged on to the second computer, he can access his (Bob's) files on the first computer. (If he's not logged in to the second computer, he's prompted to enter his username and password, which then provides access to his shared files.)

Sound complicated? It is—which is why password protected sharing is an effective way of protecting your files. However, if you want other users on your network to freely access your shared folders and files, password protected sharing is not for you. Disable it to permit unfettered access to your shared files.

Next: Setting Up Multiple Users

After your network is set up and secure, you can start using it. The next part of the book examines various ways to use your network, starting with configuring your computers so that different people can use them. Turn to Chapter 9, "Setting Up Multiple Users," to get started.

Part III

Using Your Wireless Network

In this chapter

9

Setting Up Multiple Users

It's possible for a small home network to exist with just a single user. For example, I have four computers in my house and one user (me); it's still beneficial for me to network all my computers together to share files and such.

It's more likely, however, that you have multiple users on your network. On a home network, that might be you, your spouse, and your kids. On a small office network, each worker in the office becomes a distinct user of the network.

For these different users to get full benefit of all network features, you need to set up each user with his or her own user account. A user account consists of a username and (most often) a password that identify a particular user. The operating system and all networked computers recognize the username, and then allow or deny access to network functions accordingly.

Why You Need to Set Up Separate User Accounts

User accounts are necessary if you want to establish a secure network—or even a secure computer, if it's used by more than one person. When user accounts are activated on a computer or network, only those users with a recognized user account can use the computer or network. Anyone without a user account is locked out.

In addition, file sharing can be made more secure when users are assigned user accounts. Yes, files and folders can be configured to be shared with anyone on the network, but you can better secure your data by enabling password protected file access. With password protection enabled, only those users who have a user account can access shared files; users are asked for their usernames and passwords before they are granted access.

Public file and folder sharing can also be by invitation—and those invitations can only be granted to people with established user accounts. When you choose to share a folder or file, you enter the name of the user with whom you want to share; Windows then sends that user an email with a link to the shared content and enables access for that user. Other users—including those without user accounts—are locked out.

In other words, establishing a separate user account for each user on your network is smart—and safe—computing.

Network NOTE

Learn more about file and folder sharing in Chapter 10, "Sharing Files and Folders."

Network CAUTION

Although you could let multiple people use your computer under a single username, the problem with this approach is that all your files would be accessible to everybody else using your PC—which is not a good thing. In addition, you'd have to live with any changes to the interface made by other users, or take the trouble to reconfigure things back to the way you like them. Although communal computing is possible, it isn't ideal—and less so over a network.

Understanding Windows User Accounts

A user account is simply a name (called a *username*) by which a given user is known to a computer. Most often the user must also supply a password to log on to the computer; the logon procedure consists of entering the username and password, which are then recognized (or not) by the host computer.

That said, user accounts work somewhat differently in Windows Vista than they do in Windows XP. Read on to learn the differences—and the similarities.

Types of User Accounts

In Windows Vista, you can create two types of user accounts—Administrator and Standard. In Windows XP, these two account types are called Administrator and Limited, and perform similar functions.

A person with a Standard or Limited account can perform most general computing tasks, such as running programs, opening documents, and the like. A Standard-level account can't make any changes that might affect other users or the security of the computer or network, such as installing new programs or deleting important files. He can change his own account picture and password, but can't change his account type or edit others' accounts. In other words, a Standard user can only use the PC, not modify it.

A person with an Administrator account, on the other hand, has permission by Windows to perform any function, including installing programs and modifying or deleting files. Administrators have complete access to the computer and can make changes that might affect other users—as well as the PC's security. He can access all system files, create and delete user accounts, and create passwords for other user accounts.

Network NOTE

In addition to the two primary user account types found in Windows Vista and XP, both operating system also have a third account type, called Guest. The Guest account is intended for temporary users who don't have a user account on this computer. It has no password, so guests can log on quickly to browse the Internet, launch programs, and the like. Users of the Guest account can only run software already installed on a machine and cannot install any new software.

Enhanced Security with Vista's User Account Control (UAC)

One big difference between Windows Vista and Windows XP is the feature called User Account Control (UAC). As you might suspect this feature is tied into the concept of user accounts and enhances the security of Vista-based systems. UAC is designed to prevent unauthorized people and processes from taking control of a computer and then installing and running malicious programs.

In Windows XP, all users were automatically assigned Administrator status. (Although you could manually choose to create a new Limited account, the Administrator level was the default.) This resulted in rampant security problems because users could inadvertently install malicious software and spyware on their system—and that software could then take control of the PC, using the original user's Administrator privileges.

With UAC, new users are automatically assigned Standard-level access, not Administrator access. (You can manually choose to create a new Administrator account, of course.) This blocks the average user from executing tasks that could damage the system—and improves system security.

More important, Windows Vista doesn't automatically accede to all Administrator-level requests. When any user—even an Administrator—attempts to perform an administrative-level task (such as installing a new software program, changing system settings, or deleting a system file), User Account Control presents a dialog box that says Windows needs your permission to continue. The task will not be executed until the user clicks Continue.

In addition, Vista doesn't give Administrator status to software programs, as Windows XP did. In XP, any program could launch another program or make system-level changes without the user ever knowing it. With Vista's UAC, you're asked to approve any such changes made by software programs—which should cut down on spyware and viruses trying to take over your computer system.

Configuring Windows Vista for Multiple Users

Windows Vista, like Windows XP and Windows 2000 before it, is a multiple-user operating system. That means it was designed to be used by multiple users, via the use of user accounts. You want to create a user account for each person using each computer on your network.

Network TIP

If the same person accesses two or more computers on your network, create a similarly named user account for that person on each computer.

How Vista User Accounts Work

A user account in Windows Vista includes the following settings and information:

- Username
- Password
- Picture
- Account type

The first three items are self-explanatory. The last relates to the types of user accounts discussed previously in this chapter—Administrator and Standard. You should assign Administrator status only to those users who you trust to install new hardware and software, and change systemwide configuration settings.

Creating a New User Account

To create a new user account in Windows Vista, you must be signed in with an Administrator-level account. You then follow these steps:

1. Open the Windows Start menu and select Control Panel.

2. From the Control Panel, select Add or Remove User Accounts (in the User Accounts and Family Safety section).

3. When the Manage Accounts window appears, as shown in Figure 9.1, click Create a New Account.

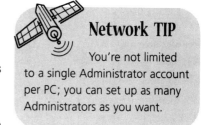

Network TIP

You're not limited to a single Administrator account per PC; you can set up as many Administrators as you want.

4. When the Create New Account window appears, as shown in Figure 9.2, enter the username for this account, select an account type (Standard or Administrator), and then click Create Account.

5. The Manage Accounts window is now displayed again. Select the account you just created.

6. By default, no password is assigned to the new account. So when the Change an Account window appears, click Create a Password.

7. When the Create Password window appears, as shown in Figure 9.3, enter a password for this new account and an optional password hint; then click Create Password.

That's it. The new user can now log in to this computer with her new user account, as well as further manage this account.

FIGURE 9.1

The Manage Accounts window—where you manage all your user accounts.

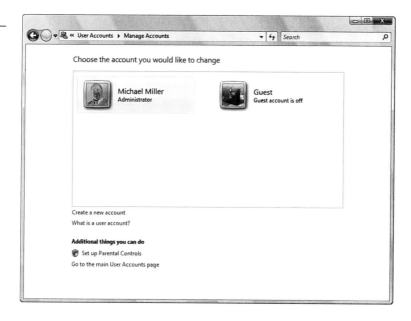

FIGURE 9.2

Creating a new user account.

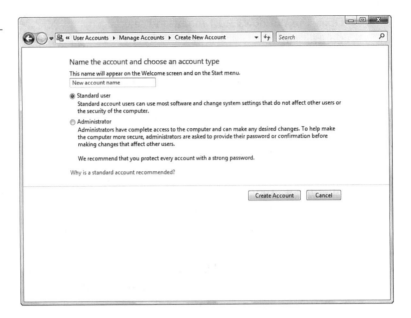

FIGURE 9.3

Adding a password to a user account.

Managing Existing User Accounts

As you probably noticed in the previous section, user accounts are not assigned passwords by default; you have to add the password later, from the Change an Account window, which you access from the Manage Accounts window. As you can see in Figure 9.4, this window is where you and the other users on your system can edit various facets of your user accounts.

FIGURE 9.4

Editing settings for an existing user account in Vista.

Make changes to Dr. Bob's account

Change the account name
Create a password
Change the picture
Set up Parental Controls
Change the account type
Delete the account

Manage another account

Dr. Bob
Standard user

What can you change about a user account? If you're an Administrator, you can change the username, password, picture, and account type, as well as set up Parental Controls and completely delete an account. (And you can do this for any account on this computer, not just your own.) If you're a Standard-level user, you can only change these things about your own account: username, password, and picture.

To make these changes, open the Windows Control Panel and under User Accounts and Family Safety select Add or Remove User Accounts. When the Manage Accounts window appears, select the account you want to edit. Then when the Change an Account window appears, select the option you want to change and proceed from there.

Network TIP

For the tightest security, every user with a user account should be assigned a password. This protects against unauthorized users accessing a computer or network by username only—which is relatively easy to obtain or guess.

Switching Between Users

Windows Vista features Fast User Switching technology, which makes it easy to switch from one user account to another without rebooting your computer. All the open programs, documents, and settings for the first user are automatically stored when you switch to a second user; when you switch back, the first user's programs, documents, and settings reappear just as they were before the switch.

To switch from one user to another, open the Windows Start menu, click the right arrow at the bottom right of the menu next to the lock button, and then select Switch User. When prompted, select the user you want to switch to.

And here's a nice thing about Windows user accounts. Whichever interface, desktop, and file configuration one user makes sticks with that user. When you switch from user A to user B, the Windows desktop and settings change to reflect the user change. User B doesn't have to suffer with user A's crummy desktop background and color choices; the user account contains all the configuration settings for the given user.

Network CAUTION

Before you switch users, make sure to save any files you're currently using.

In addition, each user account has its own Documents, Pictures, and Music folders. When user A opens his Pictures folder, he sees his own digital photos; when user B switches accounts and opens her Pictures folder, she sees her own photos. Windows is nice that way.

Configuring Windows XP for Multiple Users

Configuring multiple users in Windows XP is similar to the same process in Windows Vista.

Creating a New User Account

To create a new user account in Windows XP, you must be signed in with an Administrator-level account. You then follow these steps:

1. Open the Windows Start menu and select Control Panel.

2. From the Control Panel, select User Accounts.

3. When the User Accounts window appears, as shown in Figure 9.5, select Create a New Account.

4. When the next screen appears, as shown in Figure 9.6, enter a username for the new account and then click Next.

5. When the next screen appears, as shown in Figure 9.7, select the account type—Computer Administrator or Limited—then click Create Account.

6. The User Accounts window is now displayed again. Select the account you just created.

7. When the next window appears, click Create a Password.

8. When the Create a Password screen appears, as shown in Figure 9.8, enter a password for this new account and an optional password hint; then click Create Password.

That's it. The new account is now set up and ready to use.

FIGURE 9.5

Manage all your
Windows XP user
accounts from the
User Accounts
window.

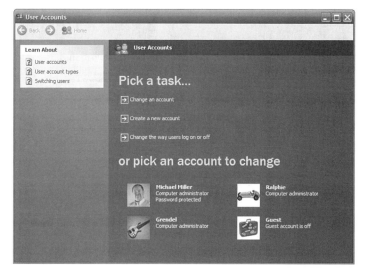

FIGURE 9.6

Entering a user-
name for the new
account.

FIGURE 9.7

Selecting the new
account type.

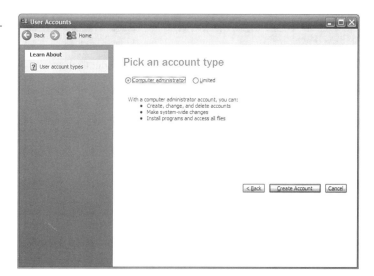

FIGURE 9.8

Adding a password to the new user account.

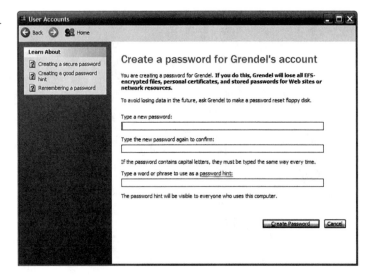

Managing Existing User Accounts

As with Windows Vista, you can edit all your Windows XP user accounts anytime after they've been created. All you have to do is open the User Accounts window and select the account you want to edit. Windows XP now displays the What Do You Want to Change window, shown in Figure 9.9. From here you can change the username, password, picture, and (if you're an Administrator) account type. This window can even be used to delete an account—again, assuming you're an Administrator.

FIGURE 9.9

Editing settings for an existing user account in Windows XP.

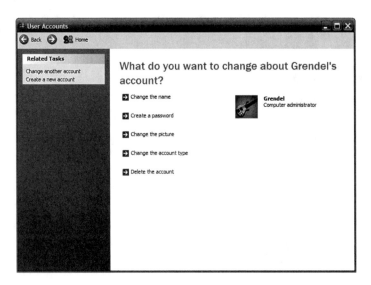

Switching Between Users

Windows XP, like Windows Vista, features Fast User Switching so you can quickly and easily switch from one user account to another. All you have to do is open the Windows Start menu and click Log Off; when prompted, click Switch User, and then select a new user to log back on with. Repeat this procedure to switch to the original or another user.

Network CAUTION

Before you switch users, make sure to save any files you're currently using.

Where User Data Is Stored

When you create a user account in Windows Vista, a folder for that user is created in the C:\Users folder. (Although only administrators can see the folders for other users.) As you can see in Figure 9.10, when you have multiple users on a system, there are multiple folders in the Users folder—including a single Public folder for all shared files on this computer.

Network NOTE

In Windows XP, user folders are stored in the C:\Documents and Settings folder.

FIGURE 9.10

Folders for different users in the Users folder.

Within each user's folder are a series of folders common to all such user folders—Documents, Music, Pictures, Videos, Downloads, and the like. This is how Vista stores the documents for each user. (For example, each user's digital photo files are stored in their respective Pictures folders.) You can manage the files for any user by going to that user's folders within the Users folder.

Network NOTE

Also stored within a user's main folder are all the configuration settings related to that person's user account. This includes Internet Explorer favorites, Outlook configuration settings, and the like.

Next: Sharing Files and Folders

User folders contained within the Users folder, except for the user's Public folder, are not by default shared folders. In Windows Vista, you probably want to place all shared documents in the user's Public folder; this folder will be visible to all other users on this computer and across the network, assuming you enable file and folder sharing on this PC. Alternately, you can configure any user folder as a shared folder, but that requires more work.

We'll discuss all of this file sharing stuff in much more depth in Chapter 10, "Sharing Files and Folders." Turn the page to learn more!

In this chapter

10

Sharing Files and Folders

When you have multiple computers connected across a network, you can start sharing your resources between your computers. You can share many different types of resources, but the most common are data files—your documents, photos, digital music, and other files that you store on your PCs.

To share files across the network, you have to enable file sharing on each of your PCs. That's what we'll talk about in this chapter.

How File Sharing Works

Just because you have multiple PCs connected to your home network doesn't mean that the contents of each of the PCs will be automatically visible to each other. In fact, all of the contents of a PC are hidden from other users by default—so you *can't* view or share files. (It's a security thing.)

If you want other users on your network to be able to view or edit a document on one of your computers, you must enable file sharing for that particular file. There are two ways to do this.

If you want to share a single document on a Windows Vista PC, the easiest way to proceed is to save that document to the Public folder on your hard disk. This folder is, by default, accessible to every user on this computer, as well as every user on the network.

Windows also lets you configure any other folder or drive on a given computer as a shared folder/drive. That way another user could go directly to your Documents or Music folders, for example, without you first having to move the shared file to your Public folder.

After file sharing has been enabled for a given folder, all the other computers on your network can see the drive or folder you decided to share. When you open the Network Explorer or My Network Places folder on another computer, you'll see the shared drive/folder displayed.

You should also make sure that you have a firewall installed on your network and that you've activated adequate wireless security (if you have a wireless network). This will keep unwanted intruders from hacking into your network—and gaining unauthorized access to your private files.

Network CAUTION

Although it's great to share files across two or more PCs on your network, you should be cautious about enabling file sharing. When you let a folder or drive be shared, anyone accessing your network can access the contents of that folder or drive. Make sure that you share only those folders and drives you want to share, and keep the other folders on your computer private.

Configuring File Sharing in Windows Vista

Before you can share files and folders in Windows Vista, even the Public folder, you first have to enable file sharing on a given PC. If file sharing is *not* enabled, no files or folders will be visible to other computers on the network.

Enabling File Sharing

To enable file sharing in Windows Vista, do the following:

1. Open the Windows Start menu and select Control Panel.

2. From the Control Panel, select Network and Internet.

3. When the Network and Internet window appears, select Network and Sharing Center.

4. In the Network and Sharing Center window, shown in Figure 10.1, click the down arrow in the File Sharing section.

5. Select the Turn On File Sharing option.

6. Click Apply.

Network NOTE

In Windows XP, file and folder sharing is enabled on a folder-by-folder or drive-by-drive basis. See the "Sharing Folders and Drives in Windows XP" section, later in this chapter, for more information.

FIGURE 10.1

Enabling file sharing in Windows Vista.

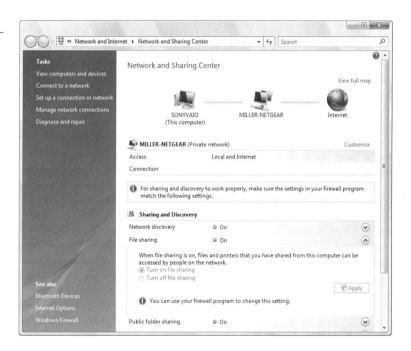

Enabling Password-Protected Sharing

With standard Windows Vista file sharing, any user on your network can access any shared folder, no questions asked. You may, however, want to limit access to only those users who have valid user accounts on your network. To do this, Windows Vista includes a new security feature called password-protected sharing.

With password-protected sharing, no one can access your shared folders, including the Public folder, without first providing a valid username and password. Even more stringent, the username must be registered on the same computer on which the shared folder is hosted; a user on another computer who does not have a user account on the folder's computer will not be able to gain access.

If a user tries to access a password-protected folder, he will automatically gain access if he has a user account on that computer and is signed in under that user account. If not, the user will be prompted for his username and password; entering a valid username and password gains access to the folder. If the user does not enter a username and password that is registered on the folder's computer, access is denied.

Password protection is applied to all the shared folders on a computer, not just selected folders. To enable password-protected sharing, follow these steps:

1. Open the Windows Start menu and select Control Panel.
2. From the Control Panel, select Network and Internet, and then select Network and Sharing Center.
3. In the Network and Sharing Center window, click the down arrow in the Password Protected Sharing section.
4. Select the Turn On Password Protected Sharing option.
5. Click Apply.

Again, for password-protected sharing to work, each user must have an account registered on the computer that holds the shared files. So, for example, a user named Bob has an account on computer number two but not on computer number one. When he tries to access a shared folder on computer number one, he'll be denied access.

For that reason, you probably want to create user accounts for all users on all your computers. Back to our Bob example, you'd want to create a user account for Bob on both computer number one and computer number two. Then, when Bob tries to access the first computer from the second, his account will be recognized and file access will be granted.

Sharing the Public Folder

The easiest way to share files in Windows Vista is to move or copy the files you want to share into the Public folder. Other users across the network can then access the Public folder as a shared folder, and all the contents within.

For this to work, however, you first have to enable public folder sharing on each of your network PCs. To do this, follow these steps:

1. Open the Windows Start menu and select Control Panel.

2. From the Control Panel, select Network and Internet, and then select Network and Sharing Center.

3. In the Network and Sharing Center window, click the down arrow in the Public Folder Sharing section.

4. Select one of the following two options: Turn On Sharing So Anyone with Network Access Can Open Files (to let other users view but not change or delete files) or Turn On Sharing So Anyone with Network Access can Open, Change, and Create Files (to allow full editing access to all users).

5. Click Apply.

Note the two options in step 4. You can choose two different levels of file sharing access:

- **Open** files only, which lets others view but not edit, delete, or create files. This is ideal for view-only files, such as digital photos— and for when you don't want any changes made to your files.

- **Open, change, and create**, which lets others edit, delete, and create new files. This is ideal when you want others to collaborate on specific files.

Network TIP

If you want to copy files to another computer's Public folder, you'll need to choose the open, change, and create option for the second computer—or the copied files can't be created on that PC.

Sharing Other Folders

Using the Public folder is the easiest way to share files in Windows Vista, but not the only way. It's a little more involved, but you can designate any folder in Windows Vista as a shared folder; this lets other users on the network access any folder you specify, without having to move files into the Public folder.

To enable file sharing for a specific folder, follow these steps:

1. First, enable file sharing for your entire computer as described in "Configuring File Sharing in Windows Vista" earlier in this chapter.

2. Open the Windows Start menu and select Documents.

3. From the Documents Explorer, navigate to (but don't open) the folder you want to share.

Network CAUTION

For individual folder sharing to work, you still need to enable file sharing for your entire computer, as described previously.

4. Right-click the folder you want to share and select Share from the pop-up menu.

5. If you have password-protected sharing enabled, the File Sharing window, shown in Figure 10.2, will list all the users on this machine in the pull-down Add list. Select one or more users from this list with whom you want to share this folder; then click the Add button to add them to your share list.

6. Pull down the Permission Level list next to each user and select a specific level— Reader, Contributor, Co-Owner, or (if you've created the folder) Owner.

7. Click the Share button.

Network NOTE

A Reader can only read files, not edit them. Contributors can view, change, add, or delete only the individual files they add. Co-Owners and Owners can view, change, add or delete any files in the shared folder.

FIGURE 10.2

Selecting users with whom to share this folder.

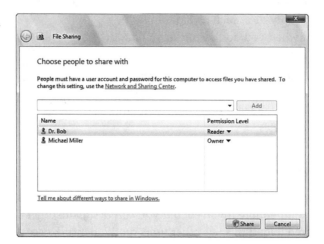

You can also enable file sharing from a folder's Properties dialog box, shown in Figure 10.3. Right-click the folder in any Explorer window and select Properties; when the Properties dialog box appears, select the Sharing tab. From here you can click the Share button to enable simple file sharing (everyone allowed), or Advanced Sharing to display the Advanced Sharing dialog box.

Network NOTE

If you don't have password-protected sharing enabled, the File Sharing window Add list has only two options—the Guest and Everyone accounts. Select the Everyone account to enable sharing with all users; then select a specific share level from the Permission Level list.

FIGURE 10.3

Enabling simple
file sharing
from a folder's
Properties
dialog box.

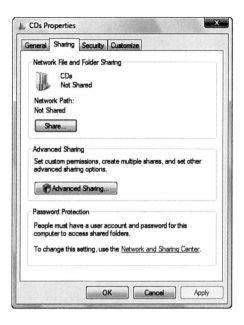

As you can see in Figure 10.4, the Advanced Sharing dialog box lets you do the
following:

FIGURE 10.4

Configuring
advanced sharing
properties.

■ Create more than one share for the same folder, with different share names.
This lets you create different ways for other users to view the shared folder.

■ Limit the number of users who can simultaneously share this folder.

■ Add a comment to the shared folder that appears to users when they access
this folder.

■ Specify who can access this folder, and their permission levels (from the Permissions dialog box, shown in Figure 10.5).

■ Specify whether the contents of this folder can be made available offline (via caching). This lets other users download the shared folder to their own hard disks, so they can work on files when they're away from the network.

FIGURE 10.5

Setting permissions for a shared folder.

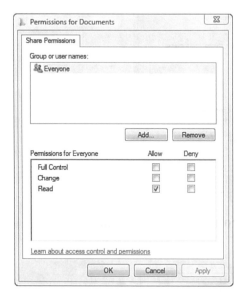

Sharing Complete Drives

Windows Vista also lets you share complete drives on your network computers—but not quite as easily as was possible in Windows XP. To share a drive in Vista, you have to give the drive a distinct name; Vista won't let you share "C:", but it will let you share "C" or "Drive C", if you can see that distinction.

Follow these steps to configure a drive for sharing:

Network CAUTION

Sharing the complete contents of a drive—especially drive C, which contains your system files—can be risky. It's better to designate specific folders to share, rather than allow unfettered access to your entire drive.

1. From the Windows Start menu, select Computer.

2. When the Computer window opens, right-click the drive you want to share and select Share from the pop-up menu.

3. When the Properties dialog box appears, select the Sharing tab.

4. Click the Advanced Sharing button.

5. When the Advanced Sharing dialog box appears, check the Share This Folder option.

6. Enter a new name for the drive into the Share Name box.

7. Click OK.

Changing the Workgroup Name

There's one more thing you might want to do to make file and folder sharing easier in Windows Vista. By default, Vista assigns your network the workgroup name "WORKGROUP." This may not be the same workgroup name used by other computers on your network; for example, Windows XP assigned the workgroup name "MSHOME" by default.

Although you can access MSHOME computers from a WORKGROUP workgroup, it might take more time and effort for Vista to discover all the computers on your network. It's better if all the computers on your network share the same workgroup name.

If the Vista and XP workgroup names are different, it's easy enough to change the name of your Windows Vista workgroup. Just follow these steps:

Network TIP

To view the name of your Vista workgroup, open the Start menu, right-click Computer, and then click Properties; the workgroup name is displayed in the resulting System window. To view the name of a Windows XP workgroup, open the Start menu, right-click My Computer, and then click Properties; when the System Properties dialog box appears, select the Computer Name tab to view the workgroup name.

1. Open the Start menu, right-click Computer, and select Properties.

2. When the System window appears, click Change Settings.

3. When the System Properties dialog box appears, select the Computer Name tab, shown in Figure 10.6; this shows the name of the current workgroup.

4. Click the Change button.

5. When the Computer Name Changes dialog box appears, as shown in Figure 10.7, enter the name of your XP workgroup into the Workgroup field and then click OK.

6. When you see the "welcome" message box, click OK.

7. When prompted to restart your computer, click OK.

FIGURE 10.6

Viewing the name of the current workgroup.

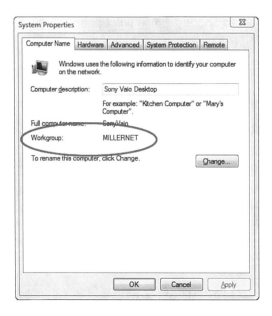

FIGURE 10.7

Changing the name of your Windows Vista workgroup.

Sharing Folders and Drives in Windows XP

As you've just seen, file sharing in Windows Vista is somewhat different than it is in Windows XP. If you have a Windows XP computer on your network, you can opt to share specific folders and drives, with no general file sharing option to enable. (And no password protection, either.) Read on to learn more.

Sharing a Specific Folder

Windows XP lets you enable sharing on a folder-by-folder basis; you share only those folders that you need to. To turn on sharing for a specific folder (and all the subfolders within that folder), follow these steps:

1. Open the Windows Start menu and select My Documents.

2. From the My Documents window, navigate to but don't open the folder that contains the files you want to share.

3. Right-click the folder icon and select Sharing and Security from the pop-up menu.

4. When the Properties dialog box appears, as shown in Figure 10.8, select the Sharing tab.

FIGURE 10.8

Enabling file sharing for a Windows XP folder.

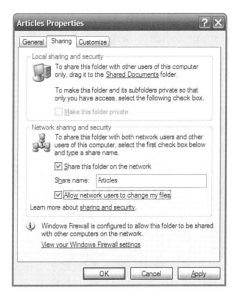

5. In the Network Sharing and Security section of this tab, check the Share This Folder on the Network option.

6. If you want other users on the network to be able to save files to this hard drive, check the Allow Network Users to Change My Files option. If you want other users to only read the files on this drive, without making changes, don't check this option.

7. If you want to name this folder something other than what it's currently named, enter a new name into the Share Name field.

8. Click OK when done.

Naturally, you need to repeat these steps for every folder you want to share on every Windows XP computer connected to your network.

Sharing a Complete Drive

In other instances, you may want all the contents of a PC's hard drive to be available to other PCs on your network. Here's how you do it in Windows XP:

1. Open the Windows Start menu and select My Computer.

2. When My Computer opens, right-click the icon for the drive you want to share; then select Sharing and Security from the pop-up menu.

3. When the Properties dialog box appears, select the Sharing tab.

4. If you're trying to share the root drive (typically drive C:) on your PC, you'll see a message telling you that doing so is not recommended. To proceed, click the If You Understand the Risk... link.

5. In the Network Sharing and Security section of the Sharing tab, check the Share This Folder on the Network option.

6. If you want other users on the network to be able to save files to this hard drive, check the Allow Network Users to Change My Files option. If you want other users to only read the files on this drive, without making changes, don't check this option.

7. If you want to name this folder something other than its default name, enter a new name into the Share Name field.

8. Click OK when done.

Accessing Shared Folders

After you've enabled file sharing and selected which folders you want to share, you can start accessing files and folders across your network. Here's how it's done.

Viewing Shared Folders in Windows Vista

In Windows Vista, all your network computers and shared folders are found in the Network Explorer window. To open this window, open the Start menu and select Network.

As you can see in Figure 10.9, all your network PCs are shown in the Network Explorer window. To access a shared drive or folder on a given PC, simply double-click the icon for that PC.

Network CAUTION

When you first add a Windows XP PC or shared folder to your network, it may take up to 10 or 15 minutes to be discovered by your Vista PC and show up in the Network window.

FIGURE 10.9

Access all net-
work computers
from Vista's
Network Explorer.

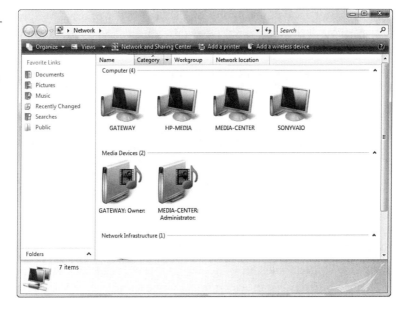

The shared folders, drives, and printers on that PC are then displayed in the window, as shown in Figure 10.10. As you can see, the icons for the shared folders look
like regular folders but with a green "pipe" beneath. (This is supposed to signify the
network connection.)

FIGURE 10.10

Viewing the
shared folders on
a networked PC.

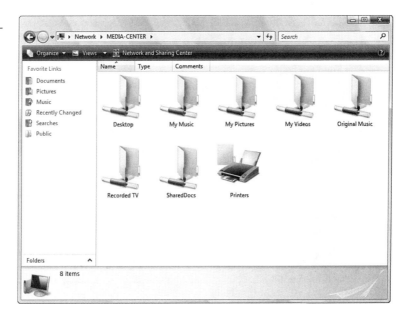

To view and access the contents of a shared folder or drive, simply double-click the item's icon. If the item is not password protected, you'll gain immediate access. If the item is password protected, one of two things will happen:

- If you're logged on to your current PC with a user account that also exists on the other PC, you'll gain immediate access to the folder or file.

- If you're not logged on to your current PC with a user account that also exists on the other PC, you'll be prompted for your username and password. Successfully enter those and you'll gain access to the folder or file.

It's also possible that the shared folder has been created with a list of specific users who can gain access. If you're on the list, you'll be able to open the folder; if not, access will be denied.

Viewing Shared Folders in Windows XP

Viewing shared folders in Windows XP is a little different than in Windows Vista. The first difference is in which folder you use; instead of Vista's Network Explorer, XP uses the My Network Places window.

To open this window, open the Start menu and select My Network Places. As you can see in Figure 10.11, My Network Places doesn't show your networked computers; instead, it shows all the shared folders and drives on your network. Double-click an icon for a shared folder or drive, and the contents of that item will be displayed.

FIGURE 10.11

Viewing shared folders in Windows XP.

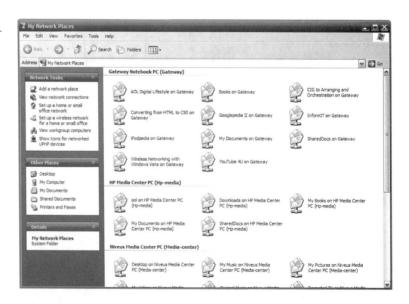

If a shared folder or drive is not automatically displayed in My Network Places, you can manually add that item to the window. Here's what you need to do:

1. From the My Network Places window, click Add a Network Place (in the Network Tasks panel).

2. This opens the Add Network Place Wizard. Click Next to proceed.

3. When the next screen appears, select Choose Another Network Location and then click Next.

4. When the next screen appears, click the Browse button.

5. When the Browse dialog box appears, select My Network Places, Microsoft Windows Network, Mshome, *Computer*, *Drive*, *Folder* to select a specific shared folder. Click OK to proceed.

6. The path of the shared item should now be displayed in the wizard window. Click Next to add the item to My Network Places.

The selected folder should now appear in the My Network Places window.

Backing Up Your Data Across a Network

Another advantage of network-based file sharing is being able to back up your valuable data across your network. Obviously, you want to back up data to a different drive than where it normally resides; this way, if the drive fails, you can restore the data from the backup drive. This backup drive can be an external hard drive connected to the same PC, or a drive (internal or external) connected to another PC on your network.

Given the convenience of transferring data across a network, it makes sense to use another computer on your network as a backup computer. You can back up to a given folder on that computer's internal hard drive, or to an external hard drive connected to that computer. Simply select the second computer (and the proper drive) as the backup device in your backup program.

Using Vista's Backup and Restore Center

Windows Vista includes a new Backup and Restore Center utility that makes it easy to back up your data across a network. To access this utility, open the Start menu and select All Programs, Accessories, System Tools, Backup Status and Configuration.

As you can see in Figure 10.12, the Backup utility lets you both back up and restore files on the current PC. To configure the utility, select Change Backup Settings; this starts the Back Up Files Wizard, shown in Figure 10.13, which you use to determine which files you want to back up and where you want to back them up to. To back up to another location on your network, check the On a Network option and then browse for a computer, disk, and folder.

FIGURE 10.12
Using Windows
Vista's Backup
and Restore
Center for net-
work backup.

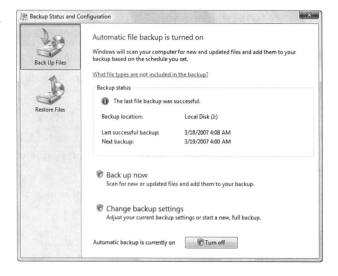

FIGURE 10.13
Configuring a
Windows Vista
backup.

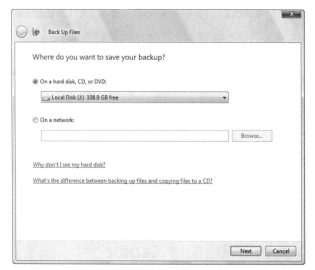

Backing Up to a Network Attached Storage Device

Alternately, you can use a *network attached storage* (NAS) drive as your backup drive. An NAS drive is a freestanding hard disk that can be connected to your network independent of a computer, typically via Ethernet directly to your network router. Select the NAS drive as your backup drive, and then copy files across your network from any computer to the NAS drive.

Network NOTE

Learn more about network attached storage devices in Chapter 16, "Upgrading Your Wireless Network."

Next: Sharing Digital Media

A computer network lets you share all types of files between your connected computers. But sharing digital media files (music, movies, and photos) is particularly rewarding—and somewhat challenging. When you want to listen to music in your living room that you have stored on your office PC, you need the information presented in Chapter 11, "Sharing Music, Movies, and Other Digital Media." Turn the page to find out more!

In this chapter

Sharing Music, Movies, and Other Digital Media

Word and Excel documents aren't the only kinds of files you can share over a network. More and more users are using their home networks to share digital media files—music, videos, and photos—between multiple PCs in their home.

Digital media files are typically large files that take up a lot of disk space. If you have a large library of digital music or digital photos, you don't want to duplicate that collection on every PC in your home. A better solution is to designate one PC (with a big hard disk) as your library PC, and then let other PCs on the network share those library files over the network.

Especially appealing is the ability to store your digital music and movies on a large-capacity office PC, but then play those files on a PC connected to your living room home entertainment system. Again, your home network facilitates this type of media file sharing, and helps you extend the enjoyment of all the music tracks and videos you've downloaded from the Internet or ripped from CD.

Sharing Media Across a Network with Windows Media Player

Network NOTE
Windows Media Player 11 is included by default in Windows Vista. To download Windows Media Player 11 for Windows XP, go to www.microsoft.com/windows/windowsmedia/. (The download is free.)

Microsoft recognized the growing desire to share media files across a network and added some unique streaming media features to version 11 of Windows Media Player (WMP), shown in Figure 11.1. That's right, you can stream music, movies, and photos stored on any PC on your network to any other PC on your network, no additional equipment or software necessary.

FIGURE 11.1
Windows Media Player 11 enables network-based media sharing.

The way WMP's media sharing works is that the original file always stays on the host PC but is played by the version of WMP on the second PC. This playback *streams* the audio or video across your network from one PC to another—thus the use of the terms *streaming audio* and *streaming video*. (Or just *streaming media*, to encompass it all.)

This media streaming is made possible due to technology called Windows Media Connect (WMC). WMC uses the Universal Plug and Play protocol for

Network NOTE
The versions of WMC built into Windows Media Player 11 and Windows Vista incorporate the Windows Media Player Network Sharing Services (WMPNSS) protocol for accessing local media content via a remote client.

discovery of compatible devices on the network. Any WMC-enabled device (computer or digital media hub) can access music, movies, and photos stored on a compatible Windows-based computer.

What You Need to Share Your Media

You probably already have everything you need to share your media on a Windows-based network. Here's the list:

- A main PC with a big enough hard disk to store all your media files, running Windows Vista or Windows XP and Windows Media Player 11.

- A second PC connected to your television set and audio receiver in your home entertainment system, running Windows Vista and Windows Media Player 11.

- Alternately, the second PC can be replaced by a digital media hub device or an Xbox 360 system (as discussed in the "Sharing Media with a Digital Media Hub" section, later in this chapter).

- A wireless (or wired) network connecting the two computers or devices.

That's it—except for your media files, of course.

What You Can Share

Windows Media Player lets you share three primary types of media—audio, video, and image files. Table 11.1 details the specific types and file extensions you can share.

Table 11.1 Sharable Media Types in Windows Media Player.

Type of Media File	Allowable File Extensions
Music	AIF, AIFF, AU, MP2, MP3, MID, MIDI, MPA, SND, WAV, WMA (regular and lossless)
Music playlists	M3U (MP3 playlist), WPL (Windows Media playlist)
Video	AVI, DVR-MS (recorded TV content), MPEG, MPG, and WMV
Picture	JPEG, JPG, and PNG

Windows Media Player does *not* let you stream commercial CDs or DVDs, only digital files stored on a computer's hard disk. WMP also does not support playback, streaming or otherwise, of Advanced Audio Coding (AAC or M4A), QuickTime (QT or MOV), or Real Media (RA, RAM, or RM), or MPEG-4 (MP4) files.

Where the Media Files Should Be Stored

For media sharing to work, your media files must be in one of the typical media-storage folders— Music, Pictures, and Videos in Windows Vista, or My Music, My Pictures, and My Videos in Windows XP. These are the folders that WMP automatically monitors for new files to share.

If you want files stored in other folders to be available for network sharing, you need to add those files to the Windows Media Player Library, by configuring WMP to monitor new content in those folders. To set up folder monitoring, follow these steps:

Network CAUTION

Not all files of these formats will play in Windows Media Player. In particular, files you purchase from online music stores may be limited to playback on the original computer only; the same with files "rented" via a monthly subscription plan.

1. Within Windows Media Player, click the down-arrow below the Library tab and select Add to Library.

2. When the Add to Library dialog box appears, click the Advanced Options button.

3. The Add to Library dialog box now expands, as shown in Figure 11.2. Click the Add button to specify which folders to monitor.

FIGURE 11.2

Specifying which folders to monitor for new media files.

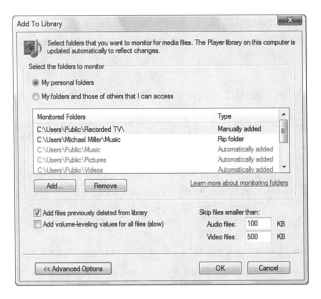

Connecting a PC to Your Home Entertainment System

To play back streaming audio and video on your home entertainment PC, you'll need to connect a Windows Vista-based PC or digital media hub to your home entertainment system. Obviously, the PC should also be connected to your home network, either via Wi-Fi or Ethernet, as shown in Figure 11.3.

FIGURE 11.3

A Windows-based media sharing network.

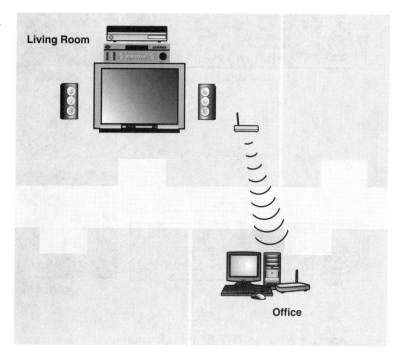

To play back both audio and video files, you need to connect your living room PC or digital media hub to your television set and audio receiver. The connections are relatively simple—if your PC has higher-end video and sound cards installed.

The video connection is made with either a composite video or component video cable, depending on what type of video output is found on your PC's video card. Connect the appropriate video cable from the output of your PC's video card to the corresponding input on the back of your TV, as shown in Figure 11.4.

Network NOTE

A strong wireless connection should be adequate for streaming music and photos. However, the larger bandwidth required for streaming video might necessitate a faster Ethernet connection to your network.

FIGURE 11.4

Making a video
connection
between your PC
and television set.

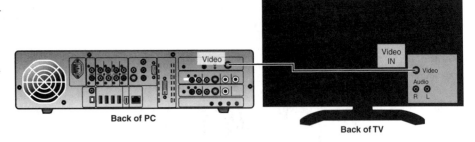

OR

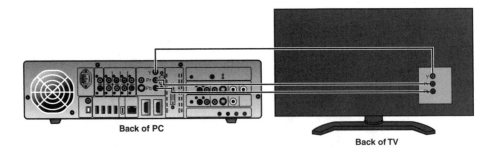

Some video cards have a DVI digital video output.
Most TVs do not have DVI inputs. However, you
can use a DVI-to-HDMI converter to connect the
video card's DVI output to the HDMI input on an
high-definition television set.

Connecting the audio is equally simple. You can
usually connect via either optical digital audio or
stereo analog audio, depending on which outputs
are found on your sound card. Connect the optical
digital audio cable or right/left analog audio
cables from the output of the PC's sound card to
the corresponding input(s) on the back of your
audio receiver, as shown in Figure 11.5.
(Alternately, you can connect the audio to the
audio inputs on the back of your TV; this lets you
listen to your PC's audio through your TV's speakers instead of your larger audio
system speakers.)

That's it. Connected in this fashion, you'll view the video from your computer on
the TV screen, and listen to the sound from your computer through the speakers in
your audio system.

Network TIP

The best video con-
nection is via DVI or HDMI.
Second-best is with three-cable
component video. Third-best is
S-Video, although few PCs
have S-Video outputs. The least-
acceptable video connection is
single-cable composite video,
although this type of connection
is okay for displaying onscreen
menus and such.

FIGURE 11.5

Making an audio connection between your PC and audio receiver.

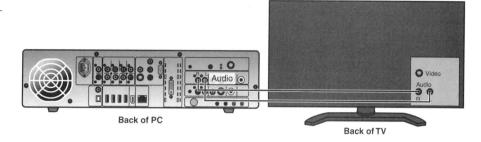

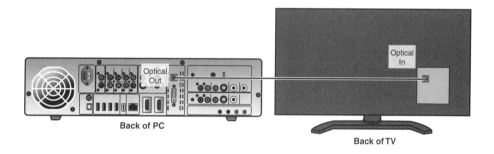

Streaming Playback Without a Home Entertainment System

The second PC in a shared network connection doesn't have to be connected to your home entertainment system. As you can see in Figure 11.6, Windows Media Player lets you play back audio and video on any PC connected to your network, using the PC's own monitor and speakers. This way you can listen to music stored on your office PC, for example, on a second PC located in your basement or bedroom.

With this type of setup, you use Windows Media Player on the second PC to open media files stored on the first PC—or vice versa. The files stream across your network from PC to PC, in real time.

Network TIP

The best audio connection is optical (or, if available, coaxial) digital. A digital connection not only provides a higher-bandwidth connection, it also transmits surround sound audio for movie playback. If you care only about music playback, the traditional right/left analog connection (with dual RCA jacks) is acceptable.

FIGURE 11.6

Streaming media files between two PCs on a network.

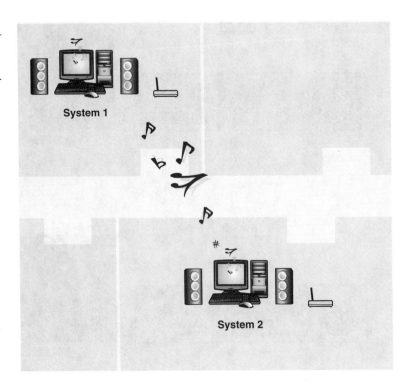

Enabling Media Sharing in Windows Media Player

Now that you know all about network-based media sharing, how do you do it?

The first thing you have to do is enable media sharing on all the computers on your network, which you do within Windows Media Player 11. Just follow these steps:

1. From Windows Media Player, click the down arrow below the Library tab and click Media Sharing.

2. When the Media Sharing dialog box appears, as shown in Figure 11.7, check the Share My Media option.

3. Click OK.

Network NOTE

When you connect a new computer or device to your network, Windows Media Player will detect the device and prompt you to set up sharing with that device. Click the onscreen message and choose to Allow, Deny, or Customize media sharing with that device.

4. The Media Sharing dialog box now changes to display a list of your network computers and devices. To allow sharing with a specific computer, click Allow. To not share with a computer, click Deny.

5. Click OK when done.

Repeat this process on all computers on your network on which you want to share or play media files.

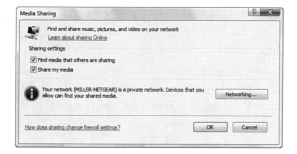

Configuring Media Sharing Settings

By default, WMP's media sharing is set to share all types of media files. You can, however, fine-tune the types of files you share. Here's what to do:

1. From Windows Media Player, click the down arrow below the Library tab and click Media Sharing.

2. When the Media Sharing dialog box appears, click the Settings button.

3. When the Media Sharing - Default Settings dialog box appears, as shown in Figure 11.8, check the Media Types you want to share—Music, Pictures, and/or Video.

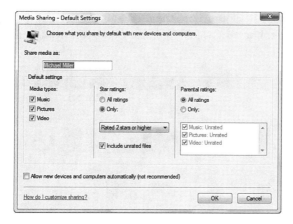

4. To change the name of this shared media library (which other users on your network will see), enter a new name into the Share Media As box.

5. If you want to share only your highest-rated media files, go to the Star Ratings section, check the Only box, and then pull down the list and select a minimum star rating. To add unrated files to the shared list, check the

Include Unrated Files option. To share all files, no matter the rating, check the All Ratings option.

6. To share only those files with a minimum parental content rating, go to the Parental Ratings section, check the Only option, and then select the desired ratings from the list. To share files with any content rating, check the All Ratings option.

7. To automatically share files with newly connected computers and devices, check the Allow New Devices and Computers Automatically option. (If this option isn't checked, you're prompted to share with new devices when they're first connected.)

8. Click OK when done.

Playing Shared Media

After you've enabled and configured media sharing on all your network computers, playing a shared music, video, or photo file is easy. From another connected PC, follow these steps:

1. On the second PC, open Windows Media Player.

2. Click the down arrow below the Library tab and select Media Sharing.

3. When the Media Sharing dialog box appears, select the Find Media That Others Are Sharing option; then click OK.

4. Return to Windows Media Player and select the Library tab.

5. As you can see in Figure 11.9, the navigation pane will now display all shared media libraries. Click the library that you want to play.

FIGURE 11.9

Viewing shared media libraries within Windows Media Player.

6. All media in the shared library will now be displayed. Double-click the file or playlist you want to play.

It's that easy. After everything is set up, all the media files on your shared computers are visible and playable from any other connected and configured computers, using Windows Media Player. Playback is automatic; the selected file is streamed across your network from the host computer to the one doing the playback.

Sharing Media with Windows Media Center

If you have a computer in your living room, connected to your home entertainment system, using your mouse to select files in Windows Media Player can be a giant pain. The standard Windows interface is designed for 10-inch operation, not for 10-foot operation.

When you want to control media playback from the comfort of your living room couch, you want operation more like what you have with your other audio/video components. That means an onscreen display with big graphics that you can navigate with a handheld remote control.

Fortunately, such an interface exists. And, if your computer is running Windows Vista Home Premium or Ultimate edition, you have that interface built into the operating system.

Windows' 10-foot interface is called Windows Media Center. It lies dormant on most desktop and laptop PCs, but it's essential for the operation of living room PCs.

Getting to Know Windows Media Center

You start Media Center by opening the Start menu and selecting All Programs, Windows Media Center. After a brief setup routine, you're taken to the Media Center home screen, shown in Figure 11.10. From here you use the Media Center remote control (available separately) to scroll up and down the menu to select any of the following functions:

Network NOTE

A living room PC is often called a *home theater PC* (HTPC) or Media Center PC.

Network TIP

To learn more about the ins and outs of Windows Media Center, check out Mark Edward Soper's book *Unleashing Windows Vista Media Center* (Que, 2007).

Network NOTE

In Windows XP, you had to buy a dedicated Media Center PC to get the Windows Media Center interface; it wasn't included in the operating system itself. With Windows Vista, however, Media Center is built into the Home Premium and Ultimate editions of the operating system.

FIGURE 11.10

The Windows
Vista Media
Center main
menu.

- **Music**—Lets you play back digital music stored on your PC's hard disk (as shown in Figure 11.11), play music CDs, rip CDs to your hard drive, burn your own custom music CDs, and listen to Internet radio stations.

FIGURE 11.11

Viewing your
music collection
in Windows
Media Center.

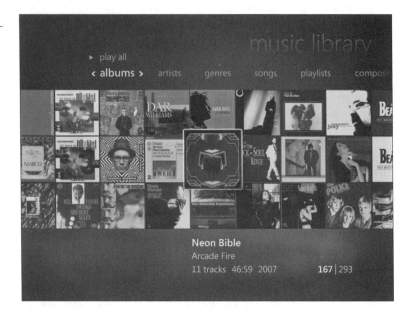

- **TV**—Lets you watch live TV, as well as schedule the recording of any television program and watch recorded programming, as shown in Figure 11.12.
- **Movies**—Lets you play DVD movies.
- **Photos + Video**—Lets you view digital photographs and videos stored on your PC's hard drive, as shown in Figure 11.13.
- **Spotlight**—Offers a variety of third-party applications.

FIGURE 11.12

Viewing a recorded TV program in Windows Media Center.

FIGURE 11.13

Viewing your photo collection in Windows Media Center.

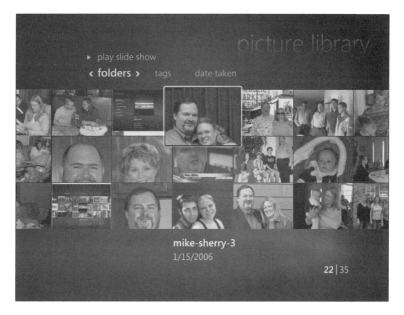

Sharing Media with Media Center

Media Center can play music, videos, and photos stored on the Media Center PC's hard disk, or shared media stored on another network computer. To configure Media Center to access shared media across a network, follow these steps:

1. From the Media Center start screen, scroll to Tasks and select Settings.

2. On the Settings screen, select Library Setup.

3. On the Library Setup screen, select Add Folder to Watch and click Next.

4. On the next screen, shown in Figure 11.14, select Add Shared Folders from Another Computer and click Next.

5. Navigate to and check the folders you want to add; then click Next.

Media Center will now add the selected folders to its library; this may take several minutes. After the folders are added, the media from the folders you selected appear automatically in the Media Center library.

FIGURE 11.14

Adding shared media folders from another computer to your Media Center library.

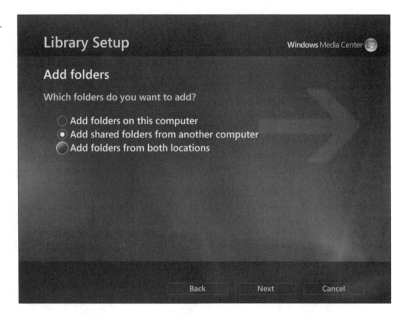

Sharing Media with a Windows Media Center Extender

Not everyone wants to put a personal computer in the living room. To that end, you may want to consider using a Media Center Extender instead.

A Media Center Extender is a set-top device that connects to your home network (via Ethernet or Wi-Fi) and accesses all the digital media files stored on your desktop PC. The Extender then feeds all that media to your living room home entertainment system—using the Media Center onscreen interface.

Choosing a Media Center Extender

Media Center Extenders come in many shapes and sizes. For many users, Microsoft's Xbox 360 video game console is the perfect Media Center Extender. Not only is it a popular video game machine, it also connects to your home network to play back music, videos, and television programming.

Dedicated Media Center Extenders are expected from a number of different companies, including HP and Linksys. Check your local retailer or the Microsoft website for the latest products.

Using a Media Center Extender

Anything you can do on your Media Center PC can also be done on the Media Center Extender. The difference is that the Extender doesn't store any of its own files, instead using the files stored on your Media Center PC.

Using a Media Center Extender is just like using a PC with Windows Media Center. You see the same Media Center start menu, which provides access to music, photos, videos, and both live and recorded television programming. Just select the menu option to play a specific type of media.

Sharing Media with a Digital Media Hub

The PC you connect to your home entertainment system doesn't have to be a PC. Instead, it can be a *digital media hub*—a device that connects to your home network, accesses the digital media files

Network NOTE
For a Media Center Extender to work, your network's main PC must be running Windows Media Center.

Network NOTE
Learn how to connect an Xbox 360 to your home network in Chapter 13, "Connecting Game Devices to Your Wireless Network."

Network CAUTION
Media Center Extenders designed for the Windows XP version of Media Center will not work with Windows Vista Media Center.

Network NOTE
A digital media hub is similar to a Media Center Extender in functionality, but it uses its own proprietary onscreen interface instead of the Media Center interface—and doesn't require a Media Center PC on the other end of the network to operate.

stored on your main computer's hard disk, and then streams the audio and video through your home entertainment system.

Choosing a Digital Media Hub

A digital media hub is typically a small and relatively low-cost device that connects directly to your home entertainment system. Unlike a PC, it doesn't have a built-in hard disk or CD/DVD drive. It connects to your home network via either a wired or a wireless connection, and to your home entertainment system via traditional audio and video connections.

Some digital media hubs are audio-only (for music playback); some are audio/video (for music, video, and photo playback). You should choose the hub that offers the features you need for your particular setup.

Some of the more popular digital media hubs include the following:

■ Roku SoundBridge M1001 ($199.99, audio-only, www.rokulabs.com), shown in Figure 11.15

FIGURE 11.15

The Roku SoundBridge M1001 audio-only digital media hub.

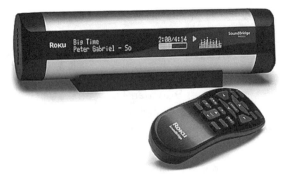

■ D-Link DSM-120 MediaLounge Wireless Music Player ($179.99 audio-only, www.dlink.com), shown in Figure 11.16

■ D-Link DSM-320 MediaLounge Wireless Media Player ($189.99 audio/video/photo, www.dlink.com)

■ D-Link DSM-520 MediaLounge Wireless HD Media Player ($249.99, audio/video/photo, www.dlink.com)

■ Linksys WMB54G Wireless-G Music Bridge ($149.99, audio-only, www.linksys.com)

■ Netgear EVA700 Digital Entertainer ($279.99, audio/video/photo, www.netgear.com), shown in Figure 11.17

FIGURE 11.16

The D-Link DSM-120 MediaLounge Wireless Music Player, an audio-only media hub.

FIGURE 11.17

Netgear's EVA700 Digital Entertainer audio/video/photo media hub.

- Netgear EVA8000 Digital Entertainer HD ($399.99, audio/video/photo, www.netgear.com)

- Slim Devices Squeezebox ($299, audio-only, www.slimdevices.com), shown in Figure 11.18

FIGURE 11.18

The Slim Devices Squeezebox audio-only media hub.

■ Sony CPF-IX001 Wireless PC Audio System ($299.95, audio-only, www.sonystyle.com), shown in Figure 11.19

FIGURE 11.19

Sony's CPX-IX001 streaming audio-only system.

When you're shopping for a digital media hub, take these points into consideration:

■ Does the unit connect to your home network via Ethernet (wired) or Wi-Fi (wireless)? Ethernet provides a faster, more reliable connection (especially for video streaming), but Wi-Fi is easier for most consumers to set up. (No cables to run.)

■ Can you control playback from the unit (or a remote control unit), or do you have to set up everything from your PC?

■ Can you connect multiple units to your network to provide music to other rooms in your house?

■ Does the unit have a built-in display or does it use your TV to display song information? (Those front-of-unit displays can be a tad small and difficult to read.)

■ Does it play audio only, or can it also stream videos or display digital photos and artwork?

■ If it's capable of streaming video, is it limited to standard definition television or high-definition (HDTV)?

Network TIP

If you're an iPod and iTunes user, you may want to consider using Apple's AirPort Express as a bare-bones digital media hub; it can stream music from any PC that's running the iTunes Music Player software.In addition, the Apple TV unit can stream iTunes-based music and video over your home network to any living room TV, something to consider if you're wedded to iPod-based music and movies. See www.apple.com for more information on both products.

Connecting and Using a Digital Media Hub

Because the digital media hub has no built-in storage of its own, it has to connect to your home network to access media files stored on your other network computers. Most digital media hubs offer built-in Wi-Fi, and some also offer Ethernet connections.

You place your digital media hub next to your home entertainment system. The audio output of the media hub (either analog or digital) is connected to the matching input on your audio/video receiver. The video output of the media hub is connected to your television display.

You use the media hub's remote control (and either an onscreen or a front-panel display) to operate the hub's media player software. You can then select which digital media files (stored on the other PC) you want to play on your home entertainment system. The selected files are transmitted over the home network to the media hub, where they are sent to the audio receiver and TV for playback.

Next: Sharing Printers and Other Peripherals

Networks aren't just for sharing software and data files. You can also use your network to share hardware devices—printers, scanners, and the like. To learn more, turn the page and read Chapter 12, "Sharing Printers and Other Peripherals."

In this chapter

12

Sharing Printers and Other Peripherals

One of the primary advantages of setting up a home network is that you can share expensive equipment, such as printers and scanners, among all the computers connected to the network. You don't have to buy separate printers for each computer you own.

After a printer is set up for network use, it's a snap to print a document from any of your network computers. When you click the Print button, select the shared printer—and your document will print, just like normal.

Connecting a Shared Printer to Your Network

The easiest way to share a printer over a network is to connect that printer to a host PC, and then let all the other computers on the network access it via the host. This type of setup is shown in Figure 12.1.

FIGURE 12.1

A single printer connected to all the computers on a network, through a host PC.

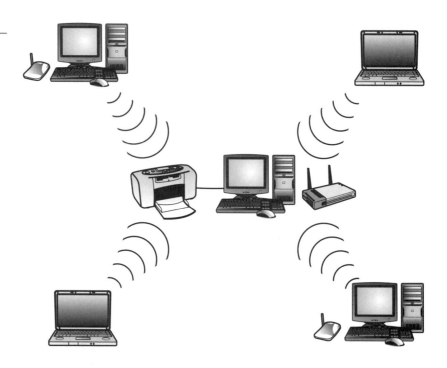

For this network configuration to work, the printer has to be configured (on the host PC) for sharing. Then each of the other computers on the network has to install that printer as a network printer.

After you complete the installation and configuration, the printer will appear as an option when you go to print from any PC on your network. Click the Print button and the print instruction will be sent from the current PC to the PC that hosts the printer, and then on to the printer itself.

This type of setup works with virtually any type of printer—inkjet, laser, multifunction, photo, or whatever. The printer can be connected via USB or a traditional parallel connection; it doesn't matter. As long as the printer is connected to a network computer and configured for shared usage, it will be available to all other computers on the network.

Configuring a Shared Printer on a Host PC

To share a printer between all your networked computers, connect that printer to one of your network PCs, and then configure the printer for network use. The process is different, depending on whether the computer is running Windows Vista or Windows XP.

Printer Sharing with Windows Vista

In Windows Vista, printer sharing is enabled from the Network and Sharing Center. Here's how it works:

> **Network NOTE**
> You'll need to repeat this procedure on each network PC to which a printer is attached—assuming you want to share all your printers across your network.

1. Open the Windows Start menu and select Control Panel.

2. From the Control Panel, select Network and Internet.

3. When the Network and Internet window appears, select Network and Sharing Center.

4. In the Network and Sharing Center window, click the down arrow in the Printer Sharing section, shown in Figure 12.2.

5. Select Turn On Printer Sharing.

6. Click Apply.

FIGURE 12.2
Enabling printer sharing in Windows Vista.

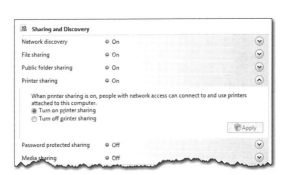

All printers connected to this particular computer will now be visible to all other computers on your network.

Printer Sharing with Windows XP

On Windows XP, you enable printer sharing individually for each printer attached to your PC. Follow these steps:

1. On the computer connected to the printer you want to share, open the Start menu and select Control Panel.

2. From the Control Panel, select Printers and Other Hardware.

3. When the next screen appears, select View Installed Printers or Fax Printers.

4. When the Printers and Faxes window opens, right-click the printer you want to share and select Sharing from the pop-up menu.

5. When the Properties dialog box appears, as shown in Figure 12.3, select the Sharing tab.

6. Check the Share This Printer option.

7. Click OK.

FIGURE 12.3

Enabling printer sharing in Windows XP.

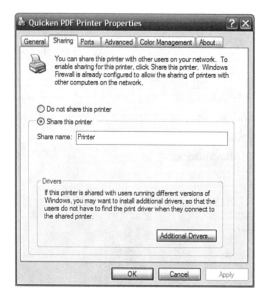

Installing a Shared Printer on Other PCs

To print to a shared printer, a connection for that printer must be installed on each of the other PCs on your network. For example, if a shared printer is connected to PC #1, you'll need to install that printer on PC #2 and PC #3.

As you might suspect, this process is slightly different between Windows Vista and Windows XP.

Creating a Shared Printer Connection in Windows Vista

With Windows Vista, you create a connection for a shared printer by following these steps:

1. Open the Start menu and select Control Panel.

2. From the Control Panel, select Hardware and Sound.

3. From the Hardware and Sound window, select Add a Printer in the Printers section.

4. When the Add Printer Wizard appears, as shown in Figure 12.4, select Add a Network, Wireless or Bluetooth Printer.

Network TIP

To set a shared printer as your default printer, open the Printers window, right-click the shared printer, then click Set as Default Printer.

5. On the next screen, shown in Figure 12.5, select the printer from the list that you want to share; then click Next.

6. You're now prompted to enter a name for the printer. Do so; then click Next.

7. The printer is now installed. Click Finish to end the wizard.

FIGURE 12.4

Creating a connection to a shared printer via Windows Vista's Add Printer Wizard.

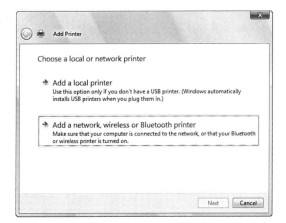

FIGURE 12.5

Selecting the printer to share.

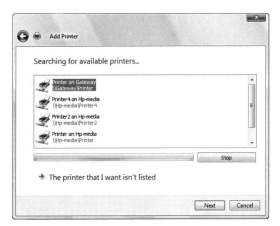

Naturally, you repeat this procedure for each computer on your network, save for the PC to which the printer is physically connected.

Creating a Shared Printer Connection in Windows XP

On Windows XP, you follow these steps to create the connection for a shared printer:

1. Open the Start menu and select Control Panel.

2. From the Control Panel, select Printers and Other Hardware.

3. When the next screen appears, select Add a Printer.

4. When the Add Printer Wizard launches, click Next.

5. When the next screen appears, as shown in Figure 12.6, select A Network Printer, or a Printer Attached to Another Computer and then click Next.

6. When the Specify a Printer screen appears, as shown in Figure 12.7, select Browse for a Printer and then click Next.

7. When the list of printers appears, as shown in Figure 12.8, select the printer you want to share and then click Next.

8. You're now asked whether you want to make this your default printer. If so, select Yes; if not, select No. Click Next to proceed.

9. The printer is now installed. Click Finish to exit the wizard.

FIGURE 12.6

Adding a connection for a network printer in Windows XP.

FIGURE 12.7

Getting ready to
browse for your
network printer.

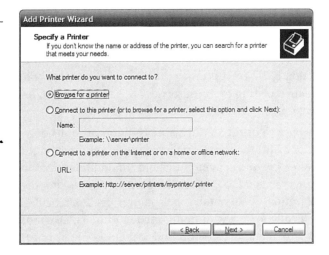

FIGURE 12.8

Selecting the
printer to share.

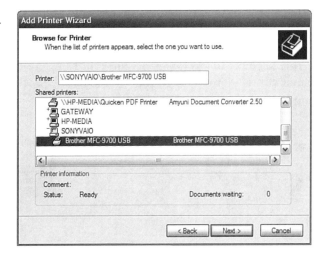

Connecting a Printer Via a Print Server

If you have a wireless home network, you might not want—or be able—to physically connect your printer to one of your computers. For example, maybe you have
a big printer that resides in your office, and your computers are all in different
rooms.

In this situation, you don't have to connect your printer to a computer to use it on
your network. Instead, you can connect your printer to a *print server*, a small device
that connects your printer directly to your network's wireless modem and lets all the
computers on your network access the printer.

Advantages and Disadvantages of Using a Print Server

The advantage of using a print server, of course, is that your printer isn't connected to any individual PC on your network. With other types of connections, your printer will only function if the PC it's connected to is turned on and connected to the network. With a wired or wireless print server, no PC has to be on or connected for the printer to function.

The only drawback to using a print server is that most units only work with standard printers, not with the increasingly popular multifunction models. (These are printers that offer fax and copying functions, in addition to standard printing.) All those extra functions tend to confuse the print server, making them unusable for those types of printers. One notable exception is the D-Link DPR-1260, which is designed specifically for use with multifunction printers. Like most wireless print servers, the D-Link model sells for around $100.

Choosing a Print Server

Both wired and wireless print servers are available. A wired model connects via Ethernet directly to your network router, as shown in Figure 12.9. A wireless version connects via Wi-Fi to your wireless router, as shown in Figure 12.10, thus letting you place your printer virtually anywhere in your house. Both types of print servers offer similar printing functions.

FIGURE 12.9

A network with a wired print server connected to the network router.

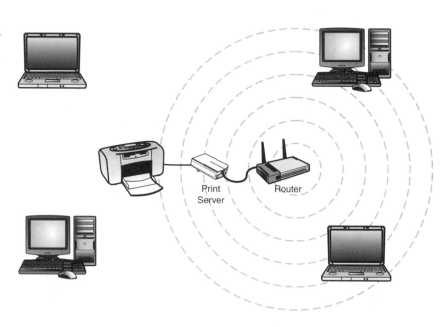

Print
Server

Router

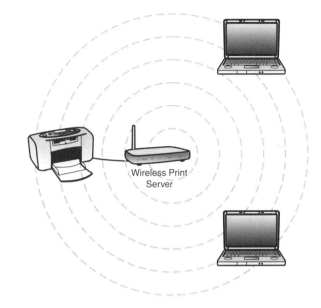

Wireless Print
Server

Wired print servers, such as the Linksys unit shown
in Figure 12.11, cost in the $60 to $180 range.
Wireless print servers, such as the Belkin model
shown in Figure 12.11, cost a little more, typically
between $80 and $200.

Network NOTE

Most wired print
servers let you con-
nect multiple printers to the
server. Some wireless print
servers, on the other hand,
service just one printer at a
time. If you want to connect
more than one printer, make
sure the print server can handle
multiple printers.

Connecting a Print Server to Your Network

Most print servers let you connect your printer via USB; some print servers also have traditional parallel printer ports. For the initial setup and configuration, the print server (wired or wireless) must be physically connected to one of your computers and the network router. After this initial setup, a wireless print server can be physically disconnected from the router for full wireless operation.

Network NOTE

Depending on the make and model of your print server, the configuration software may need to be run on each computer that is going to use the served printer.

The print server configuration differs from model to model, but typically is more involved than setting up other network equipment. For example, you may need to assign a dedicated IP address to the print server. Make sure you follow the instructions that come with the print server, and consult the manufacturer's website if you run into difficulties.

Printing to a Network Printer

After you have one or more printers connected to your network, either via host computers or via print servers, you can print a document from any network PC to any of the network printers. It's easy.

When you click the Print button to print a document from just about any application, you typically see a Print dialog box, like the one shown in Figure 12.13. All the printers connected to your network are visible in this dialog box, just as if they were physically connected to the current PC. (On a Windows Vista PC, network printers have a little green connector at the bottom of the icon.) Select the printer you want; then click the Print button.

FIGURE 12.13

Printing a document to a shared network printer.

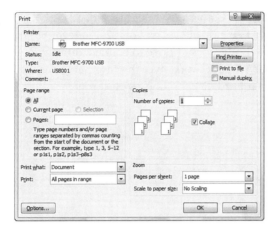

The print instructions are now sent from the open application on the current PC across the network to the shared printer—wherever it happens to be physically located. The printer prints the document, indifferent to which PC it came from.

Sharing Other Peripherals

Printers aren't the only peripherals you can share over a network. Just about anything you can connect to a PC can be shared with other PCs via network connections.

Sharing a Scanner

For example, many families and offices only have a single scanner because this peripheral isn't used that often. It wouldn't be cost-effective to buy scanners for every PC in the building, so sharing that single scanner over the network makes a lot of sense.

Installing a network scanner is just like installing a network printer. You connect the scanner to a host PC, enable printer sharing on that PC, and then have access to the scanner from any other PC on your network.

Sharing an Internet Camera

Another peripheral which is ripe for network sharing is an Internet camera, or webcam. There are many reasons you might want to do this. For example, you might install a camera in your baby's room, so you can observe your child from the PC in your office. Or you might install a webcam outside your front door to capture who-ever is ringing your doorbell, then beam the video signal over your network to any PC in your house.

Many manufacturers sell webcams for just these purposes. For example, the D-Link DCS-950G Wireless Internet Camera (www.dlink.com, $219.99), shown in Figure 12.14, connects to your network wirelessly via 802.11g technology. It configures itself automatically, so that it doesn't have to connect directly to a PC. It can trans-mit its signal over your Wi-Fi network, over the Internet (to be viewed from any web browser), or directly to a hard disk for long-term storage.

FIGURE 12.14

The D-Link DCS-950G Wireless Internet Camera.

Sharing an External Hard Drive

Many homes and offices like to share big external hard drives. This type of peripheral is even easier to share than a printer or scanner. All you have to do is connect the hard drive to a host computer, enable file sharing for that computer, and then configure the drive as a shared drive. Any PC on your network can now access that shared drive via the Network Explorer or My Network Places folder.

Network NOTE

Learn more about file sharing in Chapter 10, "Sharing Files and Folders."

Next: Connecting Game Devices to Your Network

Up to now we've talked about connecting computers and related devices to your wireless network. But if you have a new-generation video game console or handheld game, you can also connect that to your network—and set yourself up for Internet-based multiplayer gaming. Networking can be fun, as you'll discover in Chapter 13, "Connecting Game Devices to Your Wireless Network."

In this chapter

13

Connecting Game Devices to Your Wireless Network

If you're a hard-core gamer, you're probably used to playing multiplayer PC games across a network or on the Internet. Naturally, any PC connected to your network is capable of playing these connected games, but did you know you can also connect your video game console to your network—and to the Internet?

That's right, all current video game systems can go online to let you play head-to-head against other gamers anywhere in the world. All you need to know is how to connect your game system—and then you can start playing!

Networking New-Generation Video Game Systems

The latest generation of video game systems are built for online gaming. The Nintendo Wii and Sony PlayStation 3 come with wireless networking built-in, and you can easily add Wi-Fi capability to Microsoft's Xbox 360. When you go online, you can join in multiplayer games, download new games and updates, and even (depending on the game system) access news and weather reports and surf the Internet.

Connecting the Nintendo Wii

With its unique motion-activated remote controllers, the Nintendo Wii (shown in Figure 13.1) is the surprise hit of the next-generation video game wars. As an added benefit, the Wii has built-in 802.11b/g Wi-Fi wireless networking. When properly configured, the Wii can connect to the Internet via your wireless network and access the Nintendo Wi-Fi Connection service.

Network NOTE

Unlike some Wi-Fi-enabled video game systems, the Wii supports all current wireless encryption standards, including WEP, WPA, and WPA2.

FIGURE 13.1

The Nintendo Wii—with built-in 802.11b/g wireless networking.

To configure your Wii to use your existing wireless network, follow these steps:

1. From the Wii home menu, select Wii Options.
2. From the next screen, select Wii Settings.
3. From the first list, click the right arrow.

4. On the next page, select Internet.

5. On the next page, select Connection Settings.

6. Select Connection 1 from the list.

7. Select Wireless Connection.

8. Click Search for an Access Point.

9. The Wii searches for all nearby wireless routers and access points. When prompted to display the list, click OK.

10. The Wii now displays a list of available routers and access points. Select your network from this list.

11. When prompted to save these settings, click OK.

12. When prompted, click OK, and the Wii will test the connection.

13. If the connection was successful, the Wii prompts you to perform a system update. Click Yes to update the Wii with these new wireless settings.

14. Return to the Wii System Settings screen and select WiiConnect24.

15. From the following list, click WiiConnect24.

16. Select On and then Confirm to save your settings.

This procedure is easier than it sounds, mainly because the Wii's screens are relatively short and simple. You have to do a lot of clicking, but it doesn't take much time, and the process is relatively easy to follow.

After you're connected, you can use all the Internet-related features on your Wii, including the News Channel, Forecast Channel, Internet Channel, and the like. You can also access the Nintendo Wi-Fi connection (www.nintendowifi.com), shown in Figure 13.2, which facilitates free multiplayer gaming over the Internet. And, of course, you can play multiplayer games with other Wii users on your network, each using different consoles and television sets. Cool!

Network TIP

If you don't yet have a wireless network in your home, go to the wireless router rating page at the Nintendo Wi-Fi Connection website (www.nintendowifi.com) to search for Wii-compatible routers. Just pull down the Tech Support menu on the home page and select Router Info. Alternately, you can purchase the low-priced Nintendo Wi-Fi USB Connector ($34.95, store.nintendo.com/usb/), which adds basic wireless access point capability to any PC in your home without the need to set up a complete network.

FIGURE 13.2

Play multiplayer
Wii games online
at the Nintendo
Wi-Fi Connection.

Connecting the Sony PlayStation 3

Like Nintendo's Wii, Sony's PlayStation 3 (shown in Figure 13.3) has built-in Wi-Fi
networking—no external wireless adapter required. To configure the PS3 for wireless
gaming, follow these steps:

FIGURE 13.3

Sony's
PlayStation 3
game system
also features
built-in Wi-Fi
connectivity.

1. On the home menu, select Settings, Network Settings.
2. On the next screen, select Internet Settings.

3. When the system alerts you that you'll now be disconnected from the Internet, select Yes.

4. When prompted to select a connection method, select Wireless.

5. When the WLAN Settings screen appears, select Scan.

6. The PS3 now scans the area and displays a list of nearby wireless routers and access points.

7. Select your wireless network from this list.

8. When the WLAN Security Setting screen appears, select the wireless security protocol used by your network—None, WEP, WPA-PSK (TKIP), or WPA-PSK (AES).

Network NOTE

TKIP (*temporal key integrity protocol*) is another way to signify the original WPA wireless security protocol, whereas AES (*advanced encryption system*) signifies the newer WPA2 protocol. PSK stands for *pre-shared key*, the component of WPA/WPA2 that requires the use of an encrypted passphrase to access the network.

9. When prompted, enter the encryption key for your network.

10. When the Address Settings screen appears, select Easy.

11. The basic settings are now displayed. Opt to save these settings.

12. When prompted, select Test Connection to test the connection.

13. If the test was successful, confirm the test results—and start using the wireless connection.

When connected, select Network, WWW to launch the PS3's built-in web browser. You can also go online to send and receive messages, do voice or video chat, and perform other operations via Sony's PlayStationNetwork.

Connecting the Xbox 360

Unlike the PS3 and Wii, Microsoft's Xbox 360 (shown in Figure 13.4) doesn't have Wi-Fi capability built-in. That said, it's relatively easy to add a Wi-Fi adapter to the Xbox 360 console, and thus enable wireless connectivity and all manner of online gaming.

Microsoft sells its own Wi-Fi network adapter for the Xbox 360, shown in Figure 13.5. This adapter supports 802.11a, b, and g networks, but at $99 is a tad pricey. Fortunately, you're not limited to using Microsoft's wireless adapter. Instead, you can connect just about any USB Wi-Fi adapter to the Xbox 360's USB port; most USB wireless adapters are much lower priced than and just as compatible as the Microsoft adapter.

FIGURE 13.4

Microsoft's Xbox 360—Wi-Fi is optional and extra, not built in.

FIGURE 13.5

Microsoft's wireless adapter for the Xbox 360.

After you have an adapter connected, you need to configure the Xbox 360 for wireless use. Follow these steps:

1. From the main screen, select the System tab and select Network Settings.

2. On the Network Settings page, select Edit Settings.

3. On the Edit Settings page, select the Basic Settings tab and select your wireless settings.

4. On the Select Wireless Network page, select your wireless network from the list.

5. When the WEP Network page appears, enter your network key and click Done.

6. On the Apply Settings page, click Test Xbox Live.

7. If the test is successful, you'll be prompted to apply an update. Click Yes to update now; your Xbox will restart and be ready for you to use.

After your Xbox 360 is configured for wireless operation, you can connect to Xbox Live (www.xbox.com/live/), shown in Figure 13.6, Microsoft's online gaming gateway. Xbox Live lets you play multiplayer games online, as well as download new games, demos, and the like.

FIGURE 13.6
Xbox Live—
Microsoft's online
gaming gateway.

Networking Older Video Game Systems

All three of the new-generation video game systems are specifically designed for wireless use. If you have an older video game system, however, you're not left out in the dark. The most popular of the older systems can be configured for wireless use—with the proper external adapter added, of course.

The Microsoft Xbox, Nintendo GameCube, and Sony PlayStation 2 all have built-in Ethernet networking capability. This makes it easy to connect each console to an Ethernet network, but it's also your key to unlocking wireless networking. That's because you can use each console's Ethernet port to connect a *wireless game adapter*.

A wireless game adapter, like the one in Figure 13.7, is nothing more than a Wi-Fi adapter that connects via an Ethernet port, and has been slightly tweaked (in some instances) for gaming use. You connect the wireless game adapter to the game console's Ethernet port and gain automatic access to your Wi-Fi network.

Network NOTE

If any settings need to be configured for your particular network, you may first need to connect the wireless game adapter to one of your network PCs. After you've used the PC to configure the game adapter, you can disconnect it from the PC and connect it directly to your game console.

FIGURE 13.7

The D-Link DGL-3420 Wireless 108AG Gaming Adapter.

All major network equipment manufacturers offer one or more wireless game adapters. Popular models include the D-Link DGL-3420 Wireless 108AG Gaming Adapter (www.dlink.com), Linksys WGA54G Wireless-G Game Adapter (www.linksys.com), and Netgear WGE111 54 Mbps Wireless Game Adapter (www.netgear.com). All sell for around $100.

Network NOTE

Microsoft used to sell its own wireless adapter for the original Xbox console. The Microsoft Wireless-G Xbox Adapter is now discontinued; fortunately, you can use any wireless game adapter with the Xbox console.

Networking Handheld Games

If you have a Nintendo DS or Sony PSP, your handheld game system can be connected to any wireless network or Wi-Fi hot spot.

Connecting in this fashion lets you play games over the Internet, as well as partici-pate in head-to-head gaming with fellow handheld gamers.

Connecting the Nintendo DS

Only specific Nintendo DS games offer wireless play. These games are specified as being compatible with the Nintendo Wi-Fi Connection (WFC). If you have one of these games, follow these steps to connect your Nintendo DS to your home wireless network:

1. Insert a Nintendo Wi-Fi Connection-compatible game into your Nintendo DS and turn on the power.

2. On the Nintendo DS menu screen, select the game title in the DS Game Selection panel.

3. From the game menu options, select the choice for Nintendo WFC game play mode. (This menu choice differs from game to game.)

4. From the Nintendo WFC menu, select the choice for Nintendo WFC Settings or Setup.

5. When you see the Nintendo Wi-Fi Connection Setup screen, select the Nintendo Wi-Fi Connection Settings panel.

6. On the next screen, select the Connection 1 panel.

7. When the Connection 1 Settings screen appears, select the Search for an Access Point panel.

8. Your DS now searches for available wireless networks, and displays them onscreen, with a "lock icon" next to each network. Select your network from this list.

9. Assuming that your network uses wireless security, you'll now be prompted for a WEP key. Enter your network key and tap OK.

10. The DS now tests your selected connection. If the connection tests okay, you'll see a Connection Successful message, and you can begin game play.

Network NOTE

A blue unlocked icon signifies a public (unsecured) network, such as a public Wi-Fi hot spot. A red locked icon indicates a private network that requires entry of a network key. A gray locked icon indicates that this network is using a security method that is incompatible with the Nintendo DS.

Connecting the Sony PSP

Connecting the Sony PlayStation Portable (PSP) is equally straightforward, if not more so. You don't have to insert a game to set up your PSP; just follow these steps:

1. From the home menu, select Settings, Network Settings.

2. On the Network Settings screen, select Infrastructure Mode.

3. On the next screen, select New Connection.

4. When prompted, enter a name for your new connection.

5. When the WLAN Settings screen appears, select Scan.

6. The PSP now scans for nearby wireless networks, and displays a list of available networks (access points). Select your network from this list.

7. When the WLAN Security Setting screen appears, select the type of security used by your wireless network.

8. When prompted, enter the encryption key for your network.

9. When the Address Settings screen appears, select Easy.

10. The basic settings are now displayed. Press the > button and opt to save these settings.

11. When prompted, select Test Connection to test the connection.

12. If the test was successful, confirm the test results—and start using the wireless connection.

Next: Connecting to Wi-Fi Hot Spots

Not all wireless networking takes place in the home or office. If you have a notebook PC, you're probably already aware of Wi-Fi hot spots, those public wireless networks that let you connect to the Internet when you're on the go. To learn more about connecting to and using these hot spots, turn the page and read Chapter 14, "Connecting to Wi-Fi Hot Spots and Public Networks."

Part IV

Using Other Networks

In this chapter

14

Connecting to Wi-Fi Hot Spots and Public Networks

If you have a notebook PC, you may already be aware that it's becoming easier to connect to the Internet when you're out and about. That's because more and more establishments are setting up Wi-Fi *hot spots*—public access points that let you connect your computer to the Internet, wirelessly.

It's relatively easy to connect to a Wi-Fi hot spot, especially if your computer is running Windows Vista. That's right—Vista makes it so easy to connect, it's almost automatic!

Where Can You Find Wi-Fi Hot Spots?

There are literally hundreds of thousands, if not millions, of public Wi-Fi hot spots across the United States alone, and at least that many around the rest of the world. That doesn't mean you can stand out in the middle of a street and expect to find Wi-Fi access, however; you still have to know where to look if you want to wirelessly connect.

Wi-Fi Coffeehouses and Restaurants

Probably the easiest place to find a Wi-Fi connection is at your local coffeehouse. Most large coffee chains offer Wi-Fi access, as do many local independent coffeehouses.

For example, Starbucks offers Wi-Fi access through T-Mobile. Although Starbucks' Wi-Fi access is virtually ubiquitous throughout its chain of 13,000 or so stores and uniformly reliable, it's not free. T-Mobile charges $9.99 for single-day access or $39.99 for a full month's service. (The rate drops to $29.99/month if you sign up on a yearly basis.) This makes Starbucks' Wi-Fi service one of the most expensive in the country—but, as I said, you know it's there, and you know it works.

Network NOTE

Starbucks' wireless Internet service is provided by T-Mobile in the United States, and by Bell Hotspot in Canada.

In contrast, competing chain Caribou Coffee offers what it terms "free" Internet access. In practice, Caribou gives you your first hour each day free, but then requires you to purchase a beverage (or something worth $1.50 or more) to obtain a card that contains an access code for another hour's worth of service. If the barista behind the counter is particularly slavish to the rules, that means you have to drink one coffee every hour to obtain continuous "free" service. (It's possible, of course, that a friendly barista might be more generous in handing out access cards; my experience, however, has been that they're not too big on bending the rules.)

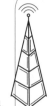

Network CAUTION

When you find a coffeehouse with Wi-Fi access, your next challenge will probably be finding a power outlet. Not all coffeehouses offer a plentitude of easily accessible power outlets—which means that you might have to operate your notebook on battery power, as long as that lasts.

Other coffeehouses take different approaches. For example, Lulu's Electric Café, a local coffeehouse in Indianapolis, uses the same access card scheme as does Caribou, but hands out the cards gratis for its customers. The only drawback to this approach is that at the end of each hour, the service stops, and you have to interrupt what you're doing to enter a new access code. A bit of a pain, but at least it's free.

Also free is the Wi-Fi service offered by the smaller Dunn Bros chain that operates in Minnesota, Wisconsin, and other areas. Dunn Bros' access is truly free—no access cards, passwords, or other nonsense required. Just fire up your PC, connect to the store's access point, and you're online.

Of course, coffeehouses aren't the only food-and-beverage establishments to offer Wi-Fi access. Many restaurant chains offer wireless Internet access, often for free. For example, the Bruegger's Bagels, Krystal Burgers, and Panera Bread chains all offer free Wi-Fi access, whereas McDonald's offers paid access ($2.95 for 2 hours) in many of its restaurants.

Wi-Fi Hotels

Most major U.S. hotel chains today offer some sort of Internet access to their paying guests. The type of access offered depends on the chain—and, in many cases, the individual location. You may find access via Wi-Fi or Ethernet; if it's the latter, the hotel probably provides an Ethernet cable for your connection. Access can also be free or provided for an additional daily charge—typically $10/day or so. If the access is free, expect to receive an access number or password when you check in.

Wi-Fi Airports

Many airports and train stations offer some form of Wi-Fi access to their waiting travelers. Airport access varies wildly from airport to airport, though. Some airports offer free access throughout the entire terminal; some offer paid access only; some offer access only in kiosks or at designated gates or public areas. You also may find Wi-Fi access (typically free) in the club rooms offered by many airlines. When in doubt, turn on your PC and see what's available.

Wi-Fi in Public Places

Interestingly, many public locations today are starting to offer free or paid Wi-Fi access. For example, many big convention centers are wired for wireless, meaning you can connect to the Internet when you're attending a trade show, expo, or business conference. Ask your event organizer what type of access (if any) is available.

Wi-Fi Communities

Speaking of public Wi-Fi hot spots, some communities provide citywide Wi-Fi access. This type of access can be either paid or free; if free, it's typically advertiser supported. (That means you get a banner ad in your web browser when you log on.)

Currently more than 300 cities are in some stage of offering or evaluating public Wi-Fi access. Few systems are up-and-running yet, but look for citywide Wi-Fi to take hold in a number of communities in the coming years.

Finding More Wi-Fi Hot Spots

Still not sure where to find a Wi-Fi hot spot? Then use one of these Wi-Fi finder sites, which list known hot spots by location:

- AnchorFree (www.anchorfree.com)
- JiWire (www.jiwire.com)
- Total Hotspots (www.totalhotspots.com)
- WiFi FreeSpot Directory (www.wififreespot.com)
- WiFi411 (www.wifi411.com)
- WiFinder (www.wifinder.com)

Connecting to a Public Hot Spot

Okay, you've found yourself a public Wi-Fi hot spot and your notebook PC has built-in Wi-Fi connectivity. How do you connect?

First, make sure you have the Wi-Fi functionality enabled on your notebook. Some notebooks have a switch on the front or side, or use a particular keyboard key or combination of keys to turn on and off the internal wireless adapter. Read your notebook's instruction manual to find the on/off mechanism, and then turn on the PC's wireless functionality.

With the internal Wi-Fi adapter working, your notebook automatically detects all wireless access points and routers in the immediate area. Know, however, that as the number of both public Wi-Fi hot spots and private wireless networks increases, your PC is likely to find more than one nearby wireless connection. Not all of these connections will actually let you connect; if a network has wireless security enabled, you can connect only if you know the network key or passphrase, which you probably won't. Instead, you need to identify the particular public hot spot to which you want to connect—which is probably labeled as an "unsecured wireless network."

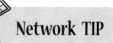

Network TIP

You can also open the Connect to a Network window by right-clicking the wireless network connection icon in the Windows system tray, and then selecting Connect to a Network. (In fact, this is how you initiate this process in Windows XP, instead of using the Connect To menu.

In Windows Vista, you connect to a Wi-Fi hot spot by following these steps:

1. Open the Windows Start menu and select Connect To.

2. When the Connect to a Network window appears, as shown in Figure 14.1, identify and select the desired wireless network. (If multiple networks appear, you may need to ask someone who works at this particular location the name of the network.)

3. Select the desired network and click Connect.

FIGURE 14.1
Choosing and connecting to a public wireless hot spot.

Because you're connected to an unsecured wireless network, there should be no network key or passphrase to enter. Just select the network and click Connect, and in a few seconds you'll be connected.

The first time you connect to a particular hot spot, you are prompted to select a location for the wireless network; you have the option of selecting Home, Work, or Public. Because this is a public hot spot, select the Public option, which applies more stringent security to your connection.

After you're connected, look for the wireless network connection icon in the Windows system tray in the lower-right corner of the desktop. This icon resembles a little computer, and should look like the one in Figure 14.2 if a wireless connection is available. If no wireless connection is available, this icon will have a red slash through it.

FIGURE 14.2
Look for the wireless network connection icon in the Windows system tray.

Being connected to a hot spot is not the same as obtaining full access; you still have to manually log on to the hot spot to use it. Typically, you do this by opening Internet Explorer or a similar web browser and going to your designated home page. The hot spot senses this and intercepts your command, instead displaying its own logon page. For example, when you connect to a T-Mobile hot spot at a Starbucks store, you see the logon page shown in Figure 14.3.

Network NOTE

Some free hot spots bypass the logon page and provide unfettered access to the Internet, no logon required.

FIGURE 14.3

Logging on to a T-Mobile hot spot at Starbucks.

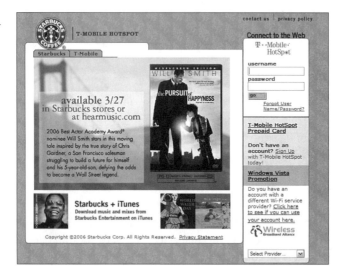

What happens next depends on the hot spot. With the T-Mobile logon page, for example, you can either enter your username and password (if you've already established an account) or click the Sign Up link to gain short-term access. Short-term access, of course, means paying by credit card, so make sure you have your plastic with you.

Logging in at other locations may be different. For example, if you're a guest at a Staybridge Suites hotel, you get free wireless access. When you launch your web browser, you see the logon page shown in Figure 14.4. All you have to do is input the PIN or access code you were given when you checked in at the front desk and then click the Login button.

Network CAUTION

Some public hot spots limit your ability to send email from your regular email program. This is caused by a deliberate blocking of access to external email servers by the hot spot provider, in an attempt to obstruct spammers. If you're unable to send messages via your mail program, but can receive messages okay, you may have to access your ISP's web-based email service instead.

FIGURE 14.4

Logging on to a free hot spot at a Staybridge Suites hotel—access code provided free to paying guests.

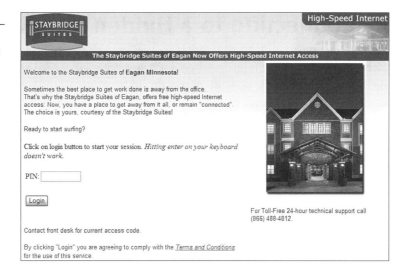

Other hot spots don't even require an access code to log on. For example, when you connect to a Panera Bread hot spot, you see the welcome screen shown in Figure 14.5. All you have to do is check the "I accept" option and click the Go Online button; no access code or password is necessary.

FIGURE 14.5

Logging on to Panera Bread's free Wi-Fi hot spot.

However you connect, when the logon process is completed you can start using the wireless Internet connection as you like. You should be able to use your web browser to surf your favorite websites, and your email program to send and receive email messages—just as you would if you were connecting from your home or office.

Manually Connecting to a Hidden Network

On rare occasions, an active Wi-Fi hot spot will not show up in the Connect to a Network window. This happens when a wireless network or access point is configured to *not* broadcast its network name, or SSID.

Just because a network isn't broadcasting its name, however, doesn't mean you can't connect to it. In this instance, you have to establish a connection manually.

To make a manual connection, you need to know the specifics of the network. In particular, you need to know the network name (SSID), what kind of wireless security (if any) the network uses, and (if the network uses wireless security) the network key or passphrase.

This information in hand, follow these steps to connect to the network:

1. Open the Windows Start menu and select Connect To.

2. When the Connect to a Network window appears, click Set Up a Connection or Network.

3. When prompted to choose a connection option, select Manually Connect to a Wireless Network; then click Next.

4. When the Manually Connect to a Wireless Network window appears, as shown in Figure 14.6, enter the network name (SSID), wireless security type, encryption type, and the network's security key or passphrase (if used). Choose to save this network for either yourself or all users of this computer; then check the Connect Even if the Network is Not Broadcasting option. Click Next when done.

5. When the next window appears, select Connect To to connect to the wireless network.

Network NOTE

In Windows XP, you create a manual network connection by opening the Control Panel, selecting Network and Internet Connections, and then selecting Network Connections. In the Network Connections window, right-click the Wireless Network Connection icon and select Properties. In the Wireless Network Connection Properties dialog box, select the Wireless Network tab and click Add. When the next dialog box appears, enter the network name (SSID) and other information, then click OK.

FIGURE 14.6

Entering connec-
tion info for a
"hidden" wireless
network.

Disconnecting from a Network

Want to sever a connection with the currently active hot spot? It's easy to do. Just
right-click the wireless connection icon (in the Windows system tray), select
Disconnect From, and then select the network name.

Note that this doesn't disable your notebook's wireless adapter; it's still on and
searching for a wireless network to connect to. This process simply disconnects you
from the current hot spot—to which you can reconnect, if you want.

Changing the Order of Preferred Networks

When you make a connection to a hot spot, Windows remembers. In fact, Windows'
memory is so good that it will automatically connect to that hot spot the next time
you're in the area, no intervention on your part required at all.

Although this automatic wireless connection is normally a good thing, it can prove
problematic if more than one hot spot is in the immediate vicinity—and Windows
chooses the wrong one to connect to. Trust me, it happens.

For example, if your hotel is located in a cluster with other hotels, you might open
the Connect to a Network window and see other hotel hot spots listed. Or imagine
you're in a Starbucks on a busy Manhattan street corner and see the option of
connecting not just to this Starbucks hot spot but also to a half-dozen other nearby
coffeehouse hot spots. In either situation, Windows might not connect to the network you want.

Here's a real-world example. I often work out of a Caribou Coffee in Eagan, Minnesota, which happens to be right next door to a Bruegger's Bagels. Caribou gives me an hour of free access but then wants me to make a purchase to get another hour free. Rather than be bothered with unwanted beverage purchases, I can simply connect to the Bruegger's network—which is free for however long I want to use it. Unfortunately, Windows sometimes connects me to the Caribou network instead, which requires a manual disconnect and reconnect to my preferred Bruegger's network.

In situations like this, you want to control the order of which wireless networks Windows connects to. You do this from within the Manage Wireless Networks window, which lists all wireless networks you've successfully accessed in the past. Here's how to do it:

1. Open the Windows Start menu and select Control Panel.
2. From the Control Panel, select Network and Internet.
3. From the Network and Internet window, select Network and Sharing Center.
4. From the Network and Sharing Center, select Manage Wireless Networks (in the Tasks pane).
5. When the Manage Wireless Networks window appears, as shown in Figure 14.7, change the preferred order of connection by dragging networks up or down in the list.

FIGURE 14.7

Changing the order of your preferred wireless networks.

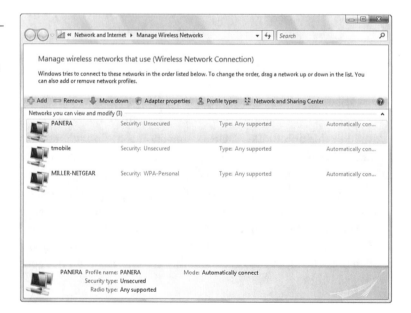

Windows connects to available networks in the order specified in the Manage Wireless Networks window. It attempts to connect to the first available network first; if a connection cannot be established with that network, it tries the second network in the list, then the third, and so on.

Working Securely from a Wi-Fi Hot Spot

When you're using your computer at a public hot spot, you need to take special care to secure your data. You are, after all, working in public, which increases the risk of data theft.

First, know that anyone in the room can peek at what's on your screen. This is the easiest way for someone to steal personal information; they just look over your shoulder. For this reason, avoid working on or displaying personal information, such as your banking data or Social Security number. And be very careful when inputting passwords; all a sneaky thief has to do is watch your fingers as you type.

Second, you should also know that it's possible for the signals you send from your computer to the hot spot's wireless access point to be intercepted. Hackers can use so-called "sniffer" programs to eavesdrop on the websites you visit and the emails you send. This makes your hot spot activities quite public, which isn't a good thing.

While you won't often encounter data thieves using sniffer programs, it can happen. The only sure-fire way to protect your data on a public hot spot is to log onto encrypted sites—those that start with **https:** instead of **http:**. (For example, most online shopping checkout pages are encrypted, as are most online banking sites.) Unencrypted data, however, can be intercepted.

> ## Network CAUTION
>
> Since you're in a public place, you should also be discreet about the words and images you display onscreen. In other words, don't look at dirty pictures while you're sitting at Starbucks. (Some hot spots employ content filters to keep you from visiting adult sites, or sites that require too much bandwidth, such as gaming sites.)

One solution to this problem is to use a virtual private network (VPN) for all your public browsing. A VPN establishes a secured private network across the public Wi-Fi network by creating a "tunnel" between the two endpoints. The data sent through the tunnel (web page addresses, email, etc.) is encrypted so other users can't intercept it. For example, JiWire Hotspot Helper is one such VPN; it costs $24.95/year to use, and you can download the appropriate software from www.jiwire.com/hotspot-helper.htm.

The takeaway from all this is when you're using your computer in a public location, most things you do online are potentially public, also. So watch what you do—and avoid sending personal data (and credit card info) to unencrypted websites.

Next: Connecting to Corporate Networks

If you lug your notebook computer from home to work, you're faced with connecting your PC to your corporate network in the office. This isn't always straightforward, as you'll find out in Chapter 15, "Connecting to Corporate Networks." Turn the page to learn more.

In this chapter

15

Connecting to Corporate Networks

Many corporate workers today are assigned notebook PCs so that they can do office work while they're at home or on the road. To that end, many corporate networks make it easy to connect notebook PCs to the network—both company-owned PCs and personal PCs brought from home.

What's involved with connecting a Vista-based notebook to a corporate network? It's pretty much like connecting to a home network or even to a Wi-Fi hot spot, but with a few corporate-related quirks.

Connecting to a Corporate Network

There are three different ways you may be able to connect your notebook PC to a corporate network—Ethernet, Wi-Fi, or remotely (from a noncorporate location). Which connection methods are available to you depend on the corporation and its network.

Connecting Via Ethernet

When you bring your notebook PC into the office, chances are you'll find a spare Ethernet jack or cable waiting at your desk. That's because most corporate networks are Ethernet networks, not Wi-Fi networks.

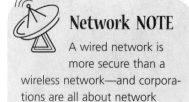

Network NOTE

A wired network is more secure than a wireless network—and corporations are all about network security.

To connect to the network, you have to connect the Ethernet cable to the Ethernet jack on your PC. When connected, Windows should automatically recognize the network and connect to it.

At this point, you may have unfettered network access, but probably not. It's more likely that you'll see a network logon screen and be prompted for your network username and password. You won't be able to access network resources until you log on successfully.

Connecting Wirelessly

Some corporations with newer networks recognize that their mobile workers have notebook PCs with built-in wireless capability and don't necessarily want to be tethered to an old-fashioned Ethernet cable while they're in the office. To that end, these corporations have added wireless connectivity to their existing Ethernet networks, typically by connecting one or more Wi-Fi access points to their wired network routers.

Network NOTE

A *wireless access point* is essentially a wireless router without the router and switching functions. It serves solely to transmit and receive Wi-Fi signals.

Connecting your notebook wirelessly to a corporate network is similar to connecting to a public access point. If the corporate network is broadcasting its SSID, your notebook should see it in the list of nearby wireless networks. If the network is *not* broadcasting its SSID (for security reasons), you'll have to manually input the network name to connect. In either instance, expect the corporate network to have wireless security enabled, so you'll

Network NOTE

Learn more about connecting to a wireless network in Chapter 14, "Connecting to Wi-Fi Hot Spots and Public Networks."

need to know the network key or passphrase. Then, after you're connected, you'll be prompted to enter your network username and password to connect to the network proper. You should be able to obtain all the necessary logon information from your network administrator.

Connecting from Home or the Road

Some corporate networks also offer the option of connecting remotely, when you're away from the office. This type of connection is called a *virtual private network* (VPN), and it lets you utilize network resources from your home or hotel room.

Network NOTE

In addition to away-from-the-office con-nections, some corporations also use VPNs for their own in-house wireless networks.

With a VPN connection, you can open and edit work files stored on the corporate network, as well as send and receive corporate email. It's like being there—but without actually having to be there.

Before you can access a VPN connection, you need the name of the VPN server, as well as your normal network username and password. You can obtain all this information from your network administrator.

Network NOTE

A VPN connection is fully encrypted, so the network data is kept secure.

To open a VPN connection from any location, your notebook PC has to be connected to the Internet. You can then follow these steps:

1. Open the Windows Start menu and select Control Panel.

2. From the Control Panel, select Network and Internet.

3. From the Network and Internet window, select Network and Sharing Center.

4. From the Network and Sharing Center, select Set Up a Connection or Network.

5. From the next window, select Connect to a Workplace.

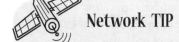

Network TIP

Some networks require a smart card for access. If you're on such a network, check the Use a Smart Card option in the second Connect to a Workspace window; then follow the onscreen instructions.

6. When the Connect to a Workplace window appears, as shown in Figure 15.1, select Use My Internet Connection (VPN).

7. When the next window appears, as shown in Figure 15.2, enter the Internet address of the VPN server, enter a name for the server, and then click Next.

8. When prompted, as shown in Figure 15.3, enter your network username and password. If you need to connect to a particular domain on your network, enter that here as well. Click Connect when you're ready to proceed.

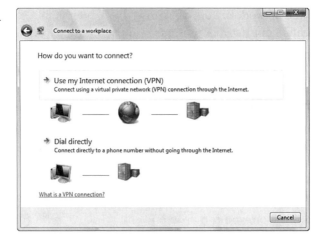

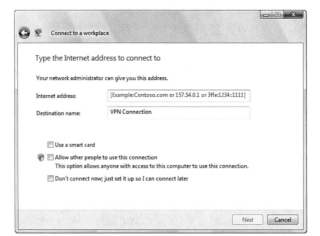

When connected, you should be able to access all network resources—files, email, and the like—just as if you were physically in the office. (Assuming, of course, that your network administrator allows full access to remote users; some networks restrict remote access to some resources.)

Network CAUTION

Connecting remotely via a VPN isn't exactly like connecting in the office. That's because VPN technology is often quite slow; you're going through several additional layers between you and your corporate network. For that reason, some users refer to VPN as "Very Poor Networking."

Connecting with Remote Desktop Connection

Windows Vista includes a new feature that makes working from the road even easier. Remote Desktop Connection lets you connect to your office computer from any remote computer and have access to all your programs, files, and resources as if you actually sitting in your office.

To connect to your work computer remotely, your work computer must be turned on, have a network connection, and have Remote Desktop enabled. You must also, of course, have network access to your work computer (typically via the Internet or a VPN), and you must have permission to connect.

To set up your work computer for remote connections, follow these steps:

Network NOTE

Remote Desktop Connection is only available for host computers running Windows Vista Business, Enterprise, and Ultimate editions. It is not available on PCs running Vista Home Basic or Home Premium editions.

1. From the Windows Control Panel, select System and Maintenance, then select System.

2. From the System Properties dialog box, select the Remote tab.

3. Check the Allow Users to Connect Remotely to This Computer option, then click Select Remote Users.

4. When the Remote Desktop Users dialog box appears, click the Add button.

5. When the Select Users dialog box appears, click the Advanced button to expand the dialog box.

6. Click the Find Now button, then click the user account you want to use for remote operation.

7. Click OK when done.

To connect to your work computer remotely, follow these steps:

1. Open the Start menu and select All Programs, Accessories, Remote Desktop Connection.

2. When the Remote Desktop Connection dialog box appears, as shown in Figure 15.4, enter the name or IP address of your work computer into the Computer field.

3. Click the Connect button.

FIGURE 15.4

Connecting to your work PC with Remote Desktop Connection.

You'll now be connected to your work PC, and the desktop from that PC will display on your current computer screen. You can access any program or file on your work PC, just as if you were there.

Sharing Files on a Corporate Network

However you connect to your corporate network, one of the main reasons to connect is to access and share data. File sharing on a corporate network is similar to that on a smaller network, although there are some specific issues you may want to address.

Sharing Files in Your Public Folder

The easiest way to share files stored on your notebook PC is to store those files in your Public folder, or in a subfolder contained within that folder. Other users of your corporate network should be able to see and access all files within your Public folder; they'll see your computer on the network and then be able to click to the Public folder.

As to your accessing other files on the network, your network administrator should set up user access to specific shared folders. You should be able to click to these shared folders on the network, as well as to the Public folders on other users' PCs.

Sharing Files with Specific Users

In addition to letting all your colleagues access files in your Public folder, you can also choose to share other folders on your PC's hard disk—and select which users have access. When you set up your shared folders in this fashion, you can even opt to send email messages to those users who have access, so they'll know about it.

To set up this type of selective file sharing, follow these steps:

1. Open the Windows Start menu and select Documents.

2. From the Documents Explorer, navigate to and select (but don't open) the file or folder you want to share, then click the Share button on the toolbar

3. When the File Sharing window appears, as shown in Figure 15.5, enter the name of the user on your network with whom you want to share; then click Add.

4. For each user you enter in the File Sharing window, choose a level of access—Reader (view only), Contributor (view all files and change/delete files the user adds), or Co-Owner (view, change, and delete all files)

5. Click the Share button.

6. Windows now prepares to share the folder, which may take a few minutes. When the process is complete, you'll see the windows shown in Figure 15.6. To email notification of the shared folder to the people now sharing it, click the E-mail link.

The user who is sharing your folder will receive an email message that contains a link to the shared folder. Clicking this link will open the shared folder on her PC. And, of course, you can share a folder with more than one user; repeat these steps to add other users to your shared list.

FIGURE 15.5

Determining who can share your folder.

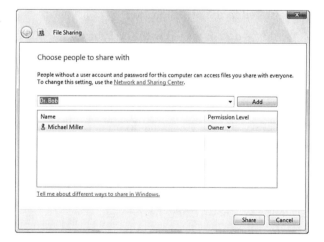

FIGURE 15.6

Your file is shared—now you can email users of the sharing.

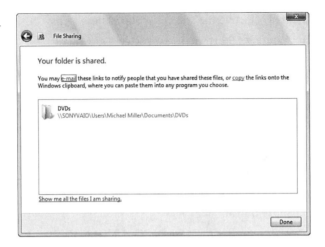

Syncing Data Between Two Computers

When you move your PC from your home network to your work network, it's easy to get your files out of sync. Let's say you have one version of a file stored on your work network and another version at home; any changes you make at work won't be reflected in the home version of the file.

You need a way to synchronize two or more versions of a file stored in different locations. When you edit the file in one location, you want those changes to be reflected in the file stored in the other location.

In Windows Vista, this is accomplished with the Sync Center. This utility keeps track of all the changes you make to selected files and applies those changes to duplicate versions of those files.

This type of file sync can be one-way or two-way. In a one-way sync, every change you make to a file in a single location is applied to the version of the file stored in the second location. In a two-way sync, changes made in either location are applied to the other file. For corporate use, two-way sync makes the most sense; you never know from where you'll be doing your updating.

Network NOTE
Although the Sync Center is included in all versions of Windows Vista, you'll need the Business or Enterprise edition to sync with network folders.

Creating a Sync Partnership

To set up sync for a given folder, follow these steps:

1. Open the Windows Start menu and select All Programs, Accessories, Sync Center.

2. When the Sync Center window opens, as shown in Figure 15.7, select Set Up New Sync Partnerships.

FIGURE 15.7

The Sync Center, where you manage all your sync partnerships.

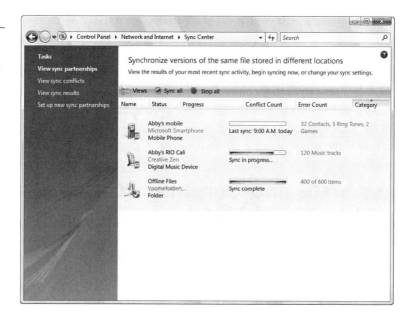

3. When prompted, select PC-to-PC Sync; then click Setup.

4. Vista informs you of various sync prerequisites—the computer you want to sync with must also be running Windows Vista, have PC-to-PC Sync enabled, and so forth. Click Next.

5. In the next window, select which folder you want to sync; then click Next.

6. You're prompted for the name of the computer you want to sync with. Enter the name of the computer (or select a previously used computer from the list); then click OK.

You've now created a *sync partnership* for the selected folder between this computer and the other computer you specified. To sync the contents of the folder, however, you have to manually start a sync or set up automatic syncing on a predefined schedule.

Syncing Folder Contents

You can choose to sync the contents of a single folder, or of all folders for which you've established sync partnerships. To sync a single folder, open the Sync Center, select the specific sync partnership, and then click the Sync button. To sync all folders, go to the Sync Center and click the Sync All button.

If you prefer not to do manual syncs, you can set up an automatic sync schedule. For example, you might want to sync all your files at 8:30 every morning, right after you arrive at the office.

To set up a sync schedule for a given folder, open the Sync Center, check the specific sync partnership, click the Schedule button, and enter the times you want to sync.

When syncing files, Sync Center compares the file versions in each location, identifies the newest version, and then copies that version to the other location. If a file has changed in both locations this creates a *sync conflict*. Sync Center notes the conflict and prompts you to choose which version of the file to keep. In this situation, you can choose to keep both versions (one under a different name), in case you can't tell which one is the best one to use.

Windows Vista and Corporate Networks—Not Necessarily a Good Match

Let's face it. If you have a company-issued notebook, it's probably not running Windows Vista. It may not even be running Windows XP. It's possible it's running Windows 2000, the previous big-business version of Windows.

Large corporations are not known for being on the technological cutting edge. You find few if any corporations upgrading all their company computers to a new version of Windows or Office the day the software is released. Corporate information technology (IT) staff tend to be more conservative in their adoption, waiting months if not years before upgrading to new software versions. That's why Office 2000 and Office XP (2003), as well as Windows 2000, are still widely used in most large organizations. They're safe choices.

Still, if you've recently purchased a new notebook PC, chances are that Windows Vista came preinstalled. Good for you. But your company's IT staff may not feel the same.

As you've just learned, connecting a Vista PC to a corporate network is pretty much a snap. That said, your company's IT staff may have issues with you connecting what they view as an "unproven" operating system to their secure corporate network. Be prepared for a fair amount of raised eyebrows, shaken heads, and muttered curse words when you show them your brand-new Vista notebook. They might not like it. They may want to "test" it on the network before they let you connect. They may even say you *can't* connect, although there's no good reason for this. It's just something they're unfamiliar with—and in the world of corporate IT, unfamiliarity breeds contempt.

That said, some versions of Windows Vista are better suited to the corporate environment than others. If you have a PC purchased through the consumer electronics channel, it's probably running either Vista Starter, Vista Home Basic, or Vista Home Premium. All of these versions have features suited for the home user, but not necessarily essential for business use. If you're using your PC in a corporate environment, Microsoft recommends either the Business or Enterprise versions of Vista, both of which offer a selection of business-oriented features without all the consumer fluff.

If you're running Vista Business or Enterprise, you get slightly more secure networking, more behind-the-scenes options that might be useful to your company's IT staff, and some business-oriented utilities and applications. All that's fine, but you can still use a PC running Vista Starter, Home Basic, or Home Premium on a corporate network. The connection's the same, even if some of the functionality is slightly different.

Can you use a Vista notebook PC on a non-Vista corporate network? Of course you can. Should you? There's no reason not to; the PC you have is the PC you use, after all. Can you? That's up to your company's IT staff. There's no reason *not* to let you connect—although that's never stopped a security-obsessed IT staffer.

Next: Upgrading Your Wireless Network

As you've learned throughout this book, setting up a basic home or small office network is relatively easy, especially when you're running Windows Vista. But there are lots of ways to enhance your network, with wireless extenders, shared network storage, additional switches and routers—you name it. Learn more about how to upgrade your network in Chapter 16, "Upgrading Your Wireless Network," which follows on the next page.

Part V

Upgrading and Maintaining Your Wireless Network

In this chapter

Upgrading Your Wireless Network

Even the best-planned home or small office network needs upgrading from time to time. Maybe you have an older router or wireless adapter and need more speed and range. Maybe you want to add more devices to your network but don't quite have the capacity. Maybe you want to add some sort of centralized network storage, or move some computers from wireless to wired connections.

All these scenarios are common. Fortunately, basic upgrading of a small network is relatively simple—as long as you carefully plan your changes.

Upgrading Your Router

Perhaps the most common reason to upgrade a wireless network is to get more speed or range. As you learned in Chapter 2, "How Wireless Networks Work," the Wi-Fi standard is continually evolving. 802.11g equipment is faster than older 802.11b equipment, and the newer Extreme G, pre-N, and draft 802.11n equipment is faster still. Even better, much of this newer equipment has a longer range, which makes it easier to connect computers in distant parts of your home or office.

The key to creating a faster and farther-reaching network is to upgrade your wireless router. If you have an 802.11b router, upgrade to at least an 802.11g model. If you have an 802.11g router, upgrading to either an Extreme G or draft 802.11n model will increase both your network speed and range.

> ### Network TIP
>
> Router manufacturers often make interim improvements to their routers that sometimes increase performance. These improvements are typically implemented via updates to the router's firmware—the built-in software that runs the router. To get the latest firmware updates for your router, visit the website for your router manufacturer.

Naturally, to gain full advantage of a faster router, you'll also need to upgrade all your wireless adapters to the matching standard. Move from an 802.11b to an 802.11g router, and you'll need 802.11g adapters, as well. (An 802.11b adapter will work with an 802.11g router, but at 802.11b speeds.)

That said, sometimes upgrading your router will provide a signal strength improvement for existing adapters. As an example, I recently upgraded my network from an 802.11g router to an Extreme G model. I didn't upgrade all of my wireless adapters, but found that my most distant adapter now picked up a stronger signal from the new router. And, of course, a stronger signal is always desirable; the stronger the signal, the more stable (fewer dropouts or dropped connections) and faster the connection—up to maximum protocol speeds, of course.

Upgrading your wireless modem is a deceptively simple task. After you purchase the new router, here are the basic steps you need to follow:

1. With your old router sill connected, run the configuration software for the new router. (You need an existing connection to register and activate the installation software, as well as download any necessary updates for the new router.)

2. When prompted, disconnect and remove the old router.

3. Place the new router in position and connect to it all existing cables.

4. Finish running the installation routine for the new router.

Naturally, if you change any network settings (such as the router's SSID or encryption passphrase), you'll need to reconfigure your other network devices for this new router. This might mean setting up a new network on each of your network computers, or simply changing configuration settings on all your wireless adapters.

Upgrading Wireless Adapters

When you upgrade your wireless router to a newer Wi-Fi protocol, you should also upgrade all your wireless adapters. If you have a draft 802.11n router, you need draft 802.11n adapters to gain full advantage of the new router's faster speed.

Upgrading a wireless adapter is relatively easy. After you purchase a new adapter, follow these general steps:

1. Disconnect your current wireless adapter.
2. Uninstall any software used for the current adapter.
3. Run the setup routine for the new adapter.
4. When prompted, connect the new adapter.
5. Configure the new adapter as necessary for your network.

Naturally, you'll use your existing SSID, passphrase, and workgroup name to configure the new adapter. When installed, the adapter should use all the other existing network settings on the attached computer; all your network places, shared folders, and the like should remain the same.

Extending Network Range with an External Antenna

You don't necessarily need to replace your router to get better network performance. Sometimes better performance can be had by replacing your router's built-in antenna with an external antenna.

For example, the Linksys HGA9N omni-direction antenna ($119, www.linksys.com), shown in Figure 16.1, boosts signal strength by 9dBi, thus extending the range of your wireless network. Other external antennas, such as the D-Link ANT24-1800 ($169.99, www.dlink.com) shown in Figure 16.2, are directional in nature. Choose a directional antenna when your router is located on an outside wall, and you want to focus your RF signals in a single direction—inward rather than beaming outside into your neighborhood.

Network NOTE

Most external Wi-Fi antennas are designed to be used with specific routers or access points. Make sure the antenna you choose is compatible with your existing wireless router.

FIGURE 16.1
The Linksys
HGA9N omni-
directional Wi-Fi
antenna.

FIGURE 16.2
D-Link's ANT24-
1800 directional
antenna.

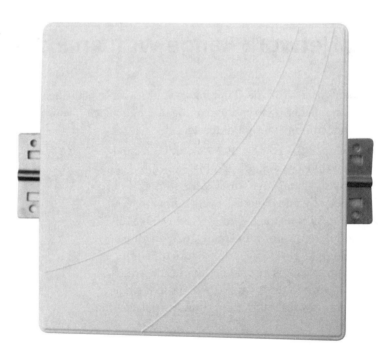

Extending Network Range with a Wireless Extender

Another way to extend the range of your wireless network is with a wireless extender or repeater, such as the Belkin F5D7132 Wireless G Universal Range Extender ($69.99, www.belkin.com) shown in Figure 16.3. An extender is a passive device that receives and then retransmits Wi-Fi signals, no network configuration necessary.

FIGURE 16.3

The Belkin
Wireless G
Universal Range
Extender.

Installing a wireless extender is simplicity itself. In most cases, all you have to do is set it in place and plug it into a power outlet; there's no network setup required. Position the extender at the farthest range of your current network, or halfway between your router and your farthermost computer. The device will extend your network from that point.

Adding More Storage with a Network Attached Storage Drive

If you have a lot of shared files on your network—digital photos, music tracks, you name it—you may want to consider putting these files on a separate network attached storage (NAS) drive. This is a hard disk drive that connects directly to your network router via Ethernet and is then easily accessible from any computer on your network. Because the drive is not physically connected to any of your PCs, it's not dependent on a computer for operation.

NAS drives are available from a variety of manufacturers, including Buffalo, Iomega, and La Cie. Prices run the gamut, from $200 for a smaller (250GB or so) drive to $2000 or more for a super high-capacity model. Figure 16.4 shows a unit somewhere in the middle, La Cie's 1 terrabyte Ethernet Disk RAID, which sells for $839.99.

To connect an NAS drive to your network, you may first have to connect it to one of your network PCs to configure the device. Other NAS drives can be configured remotely from another computer, across the network. When configured, connect the drive directly to your network router, via Ethernet. It should automatically show up as a network device on all your network computers.

Bridging Wired and Wireless Devices and Networks with an Ethernet Bridge

What do you do if you have an Ethernet-based device on your network, but want to move it to another room—and thus need to establish a wireless connection? The answer is an Ethernet bridge, a device that "bridges" any Ethernet device or network to your established wireless network.

For example, you may have a cable or satellite set-top box that connects to your network via Ethernet. To turn this device into a wireless device, simply connect it to an Ethernet bridge, which then connects to your network wirelessly.

You can also use an Ethernet bridge in a small office to connect an existing Ethernet network to a wireless network. The bridge connects to an Ethernet port on the first network's wired router, and then connects wirelessly to the other network's wireless router.

An Ethernet bridge can also be used to connect two remote wired networks together. For example, you may have one Ethernet network in your firm's office and another in a connected warehouse. Connect an Ethernet bridge to each wired network, and let the device "bridge" the two networks, wirelessly.

Most Ethernet bridges require very little setup and configuration. In most instances there are no drivers to install; all you have to do is physically connect the bridge and then run a short configuration routine. Figure 16.5 shows the Linksys WET54G Wireless-G Ethernet Bridge ($89.99, www.linksys.com).

FIGURE 16.5

The Linksys
WET54G
Wireless-G
Ethernet Bridge.

Converting a Wireless Device to an Ethernet Connection

Sometimes you want to go the other direction and turn wireless connections into wired ones. For example, you might find that a wireless connection has too much lag for multiplayer gaming, or isn't fast enough to stream downloaded videos from one computer to another. In these instances, you're better served by connecting your remote devices via Ethernet rather than using Wi-Fi.

To switch a device from wireless to Ethernet, you'll need to string Ethernet cable between the device and your network router; then follow these general steps:

1. Disconnect or deactivate the wireless adapter on the device you want to switch.

2. Uninstall the software for the wireless adapter.

3. If the device doesn't have an Ethernet port built in, you'll need to install an internal network interface card (NIC) or external Ethernet adapter (typically to a USB port on the device).

4. Connect one end of the Ethernet cable to the Ethernet port on the device.

5. Connect the other end of the Ethernet cable to a spare port on your network router.

Many computers and devices will automatically detect the new network connection and perform any necessary configuration automatically. Other devices may need to be configured for the new Ethernet connection. Follow the instructions for your particular device.

Extending Your Ethernet Network with a Network Switch

If you have a large Ethernet network, you may want to extend that network without adding wireless capability. When you need to add more computers to your wired network, you do so by connecting one or more network switches to the network. A network switch, such as the Netgear GS108 ProSafe 8-Port Gigabit Network Switch ($84.99, www.netgear.com) shown in Figure 16.6, is like an intelligent hub or router, serving to route signals from one network device to another.

A network switch can be used in lieu of an additional network router to add more computers to your existing Ethernet network. Just connect the network switch to an Ethernet port on your network router; then connect the new computers to the switch. In this fashion, the switch expands the capacity of your existing network.

Network NOTE

Ethernet hubs, switches, and routers are similar in what they do—route data from one point on the network to another. A hub is the simplest type of device, in that it blindly outputs all data to all computers. A switch is more intelligent, as it can route data from one computer to another specific computer. A router is even more versatile, enabling connections to other networks and to the Internet.

Because switches have no Internet capability, most require little or no configuration. Just connect the necessary Ethernet cables and power it up.

FIGURE 16.6

Netgear's GS108
ProSafe 8-Port
Gigabit Network
Switch.

Upgrading Your Notebook PC

The last bit of upgrading you might want to consider involves your notebook PC. Most notebooks today come with built-in Wi-Fi capability, which means an internal wireless adapter. Unfortunately, these internal wireless adapters are not typically at the cutting edge of Wi-Fi technology; at best you'll get 802.11g capability.

If you want a faster wireless connection, you need to upgrade to Extreme G or draft 802.11n technology. But how do you do this when the wireless adapter is built into your laptop?

The solution is surprisingly simple. All you have to do is disable the internal wireless adapter, typically via a front-panel switch or keyboard shortcut, and then insert a wireless adapter card into your notebook's PC Card slot. The add-on adapter card supersedes the internal wireless adapter; with the card inserted, your notebook uses the adapter card for its wireless access.

Network TIP

You can also disable your wireless adapter from within Windows Vista. To do this, open the Network and Sharing Center, click Manage Network Connections, and when the next window appears, right-click the wireless network adapter and select Disable.

You can find wireless adapter cards for all current Wi-Fi technologies—802.11g, Extreme G, and draft 802.11n. For example, the D-Link DWA-652 Xtreme N Notebook Adapter ($119.99, www.dlink.com) shown in Figure 16.7 adds draft 802.11n wireless to any notebook PC. It's considerably faster than your notebook's built-in wireless—assuming you pair it with a matching draft 802.11n wireless router, of course.

FIGURE 16.7

D-Link's DWA-652 Xtreme N Notebook Adapter adds draft 802.11n wireless to any notebook PC.

Next: Troubleshooting Network Problems

You have all the equipment. You've made the necessary connections and configured all appropriate settings. But somehow, for some reason, your network isn't working as it should. What do you do?

The answer lies in this book's final chapter, "Troubleshooting Wireless Network Problems." Turn the page to learn how to find and fix what ails your network.

In this chapter

17

Troubleshooting Wireless Network Problems

In the best of all possible worlds, you set up your wireless Windows Vista network, and everything works exactly as promised. All your PCs connect to the network, all your shared files and resources are visible and accessible, and nothing ever disappears or quits working.

I wish I lived in that world.

In the real world, however, not everything always works as promised. Some computers have trouble connecting to the network. Some computers go invisible to your other computers. Some shared folders don't show up on other computers. Some shared devices can't be shared. Things fall apart; the center cannot hold.

When your wireless network hiccups and coughs and generally starts acting sickly, it's time to start troubleshooting. Read on to learn how.

General Troubleshooting Advice

Windows Vista includes a nifty built-in network diagnostics utility, but before we get to that let's examine some general steps you can take to troubleshoot virtually any network-related problem. It's important to tackle these steps calmly and coolly, with as little panic as possible. Just remember this: Almost all problems can be solved, somehow. Just be patient and try to work things out.

The Troubleshooting Process

Whether you lose access to a shared network folder, lose your Internet connection, or have a network computer virtually disappear from the network, there are some common steps you can take to diagnose and fix the problem. In order, here are ten things to try:

1. **Wait a minute.** Some network-related problems aren't really problems at all. The ability to see a computer or resource on your network might have a slight lag from when you connect that device or boot up a specific computer. If you can't see a computer or folder, just wait a few minutes and then try again—it might miraculously appear!

2. **Check your connections.** You'd be surprised how many problems are caused by loose or poorly connected cables. If a particular device is connected to a computer via USB, unplug and then reconnect the USB cable. (On both ends, if necessary.) If it's an Ethernet connection, do the same thing—disconnect the Ethernet cable (at both ends) and then reconnect it. You get the idea.

3. **Turn it off—and then back on again.** If the problem is with an external device, such as a network router or broadband modem, you can fix many problems just by turning off the device (or disconnecting it from its power source), waiting 30 seconds or so, and then powering it back up again. For some devices, this reboots the operating firmware, thus "cleaning out" any problems that may have been stuck in the unit's operating queue or memory.

4. **Reboot your PC.** It's amazing how many problems can be fixed by turning a computer off and then back on again. I'm not sure why, but many problems seem to disappear when a computer boots up from scratch. Of course, for some problems you may need to reboot *two* computers. For example, if you're having trouble seeing one computer on your network from another computer, you may need to reboot both your current computer and the computer that's become invisible. That's because the problem could be in either computer (either seeing or being seen); rebooting both computers makes for a clean reconnect over the network.

5. **Run Vista's network diagnostics.** Windows Vista includes a utility called Windows Network Diagnostics. You can use this utility to help troubleshoot any network-related problem—as we'll discuss next.

6. **Update the drivers.** If you suspect your problem is with a device directly connected to one of your computers, such as a wireless adapter, go to the equipment manufacturer's website and look for the latest version of the device drivers. Outdated or corrupt drivers can cause all sorts of equipment problems; updating the drivers is always a good fix.

7. **Restore your system.** If your problem relates to a specific computer, and if that computer has recently had new software or hardware installed, the easiest solution may be to perform a System Restore operation. This operation restores your system to the known working condition at a particular point in the past. Open the Start menu; then select All Programs, Accessories, System Tools, System Restore to open the System Restore window. From here you can choose to restore to Windows' recommended restore point or to a different restore point. Make your choice and click Next.

8. **Restore your router configuration.** Likewise, sometimes the configuration of your wireless router can become somehow bumfoozled. Although it's always interesting to find out why this happens, it's more important to learn how to fix it. The best way to proceed is to open your router's configuration utility and look for a button to restore all settings to their defaults. Alternately, you can rerun your router's setup routine, thus effectively restoring your router to its default settings.(Note that if you do this, you'll need to enter new security keys—for all your devices.)

9. **Update the firmware.** Conversely, the firmware used in your network router may also need updating. Check with the router manufacturer's website to see whether a firmware update is in order; these updates often fix known bugs and thus correct all manner of network-related problems.

10. **When all else fails, call in professional help**. You can go through many troubleshooting routines (and we'll talk about some in the balance of this chapter), but sometimes hard-to-identify problems are best left to professionals. If you feel you've exhausted all avenues with which you're technically comfortable, it may be time to drop back 10 and punt. You can contact your network hardware's tech support department, or schedule a visit by a computer/network repair firm, such as Best Buys' Geek Squad, Circuit City's Firedog, or any number of local repair shops. These people make a living fixing problems like yours; use them if you need them.

Using Vista's Network Diagnostics

Perhaps the easiest way to find and fix simple networking problems in Windows Vista is to use the Windows Network Diagnostics utility. This utility attempts to automatically identify and repair any problems that might be currently plaguing your network or Internet connection.

To start the Windows Network Diagnostics utility, right-click the wireless network connection icon in the Windows system tray and select Diagnose and Repair from the pop-up menu. Windows will attempt to identify the current problem, ultimately displaying a window that offers one or more specific solutions to the perceived problem. Click the recommended solutions to make the fixes.

Network NOTE

Windows XP doesn't include a self-fixing utility, but does include the Networking Troubleshooter you can use to track down your problems. Open the Start menu, select Help and Support, click Fixing a Problem, click Networking Problems, and then select Home and Small Office Networking Troubleshooter. Answer the onscreen questions to help diagnose your network-related problems.

Troubleshooting Common Problems

As I said, the Network Diagnostics utility is good for finding and fixing simple network-related problems. If the utility doesn't fix your particular problem, it's time to do a bit more brainstorming.

To that end, here are some of the more common networking problems you're likely to encounter on a Vista-based network, and some suggestions for making those problems go away.

Windows Can't Find or Connect to a Wireless Network

Theoretically, if your computer has a wireless adapter built-in or attached, it should recognize all wireless networks within broadcasting range. But what do you do if a wireless network that you know exists doesn't show up in the Connect to Wireless Network window?

Check Your Wireless Adapter

The first thing to check is your PC's wireless adapter. If you have a notebook PC, make sure that the built-in adapter hasn't been inadvertently switched off. Depending on your particular notebook, that might mean flipping a physical switch, pressing a keyboard hotkey combination, or virtually flipping the switch via a software utility. (I used to have a Sony notebook with a front-panel wireless adapter switch; I can't tell you how many times I accidentally slid that switch into the off position and didn't know it.) If you have a desktop PC, check the USB connection between your external adapter and your computer.

An inability to connect to a wireless network might also be due to a faulty wireless adapter on your computer. You can check this by opening the Network and Sharing Center and then selecting Manage Network Connections. If your adapter isn't working properly, the network icon should indicate some sort of problem.

You can also use the Windows Device Manager to verify that the wireless adapter is working properly. From the Control Panel, select System and Maintenance; then select Device Manager. From the Device Manager window, expand the Network Adapters section, right-click your particular adapter, and then click Properties. When the Properties dialog box appears, look to the Device Status section to see whether everything is in working order.

If there is a problem with the network adapter, you may be able to fix it by downloading and installing the latest version of the adapter's device driver. Go the manufacturer's website for instructions.

Another possibility, if you have a notebook PC, is that Windows might have turned off or reduced power to the wireless adapter, with the goal of conserving battery power. You can check this by opening the Control Panel and selecting System and Maintenance, then Power Options. When the Power Options window appears, click Change Plan Settings next to the currently selected power plan. When the next window appears, click Change Advanced Power Settings. When the Power Options dialog box appears, expand the Wireless Adapter Settings section, expand the Power Saving Mode section, and select Maximum Performance mode. (The other modes reduce power to the wireless adapter.)

Ensure That You're in Range

Next, make sure you're really within range of the particular network. If you're too far away from the wireless router or access point, the Wi-Fi signal deteriorates and eventually becomes too weak to lock into. For a typical 802.11b/g router, your maximum range will be about 150 feet, depending on any physical barriers between you and the signal. Try moving closer to the router or access point and see whether that makes a difference.

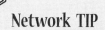

Network TIP

You can see if you're really in range by checking the signal strength for this network in Vista's Network and Sharing Center.

Eliminate Interference

It's also possible that you're experiencing some sort of interference from other devices using the 2.4GHz RF band. This could be a baby monitor, cellular phone, or even a microwave oven. (The 2.4GHz band is unlicensed, which means any type of device can use these frequencies.) If you know there's

Network TIP

You change the wireless channel within the setup software for your router and wireless adapter. There should be a channel setting somewhere on the main configuration page.

another wireless device in range, try turning it off. You can also change your router and adapter settings to use a different wireless channel; sometimes one channel is clearer than others.

Make Sure Your Router and Windows Are Configured to Use the Same Network Type

Another possibility is that Windows is not configured to connect to the same type of network that the router is configured for. Your router should be configured for infrastructure mode; if your PC is configured for ad hoc mode instead, it won't recognize your router's infrastructure network. (Conversely, you may need to reconfigure your router from ad hoc to infrastructure mode.) You can reset your computer for infrastructure mode by opening the Start menu and selecting All Programs, Accessories, Command Prompt. When the command prompt window opens, type the following command, all on one line:

```
netsh wlan add filter permission=allow ssid="name"
networktype=infrastructure
```

Replace *name* with the SSID for your network. Alternately, you can use your wireless adapter's configuration utility to make this change.

Check Your Router

Of course, this type of problem doesn't have to be a problem with your PC; it can also be caused by a problem with the network's wireless router or access point. It's possible that the router/access point is turned off, too busy to respond to new requests, or frozen. If it's your router, make sure it's turned on; you may also try powering it off and then powering it back up again to reboot or unfreeze the firmware. If it's a public access point, ask someone in authority to do the same.

Alternately, you may need to rerun the configuration utility for the wireless router. This might be necessary if the settings have been somehow changed; rerunning the initial configuration should return things to a working setting.

Temporarily Disable Wireless Security

You may also want to try temporarily turning off wireless security on the router. Turning off the firewall on either or both computers may also solve this type of connection problem. After you get connected, however, reconfigure things so that you can turn back on the firewall and wireless security.

Disable Virus Protection Software

Another possible connection culprit is your PC's antivirus software. That's right, some antivirus utilities are so aggressive they can interfere with your system's networking capabilities. Try turning off the antivirus and see what happens.

Disable Your Firewall

It's even more common for an aggressive firewall program to block access to a network. Try disabling the firewall on your computer and see what happens. If the firewall is blocking access, you may need to configure your firewall to enable access to a particular port; check your firewall's help system for instructions on how to do this, and to find out which port you need to open.

Check with Your Network Administrator

If you're trying to connect to a corporate network, it's possible that the network administrator is blocking access to the network. Check with the network administrator to obtain access.

Is the SSID Being Broadcast?

It's also possible that the wireless network may be there but just not be visible. This is caused when the router is configured not to broadcast the network SSID. If you know the network's SSID you can connect manually, as described in Chapter 14, "Connecting to Wi-Fi Hot Spots and Public Networks."

Network CAUTION

SSIDs are case sensitive. So entering **LinkSys** is different from entering **linksys** or **LINKSYS** as the network name.

Is the Network Compatible with Your Wireless Equipment?

Finally, you may be trying to connect to an incompatible network. Although 802.11b, g, and n equipment should all be compatible, 802.11a is the odd bird of the bunch, due to its use of the 5GHz RF band. If the wireless router is of the 802.11a variety and your computer has an 802.11g adapter, they're not going to be able to talk to each other. You'll need to change either the router or the adapter for compatibility.

Wireless Signal Is Low—Speed Is Slow or Connection Gets Dropped

If you can connect to a wireless network but find that the signal is extremely low, you may end up experiencing all sorts of problems—dropped connections, slow transmission rates, you name it. When you have a low signal, here are some things to look for.

Network TIP

You can determine signal strength by opening the Start menu and selecting Connect To; the Connect to Wireless Network window lists the signal strengths for all nearby wireless networks. Even faster, just hover your cursor over the wireless connection icon in the Windows system tray, which displays a pop-up information window that describes the current network's signal strength.

Are You in Range?

The first thing to check is how far away your computer is from the wireless router or access point. The farther away you are, the weaker the signal. A simple solution—if you can do it—is to move your computer closer to the router/access point.

Proper Router and Wireless Adapter Placement

You can also increase signal strength by not hiding your wireless adapter or router. If you use a USB wireless adapter, for example, it may be stuck down on the floor behind your PC, which is a perfect way to interfere with the Wi-Fi signal. Move the adapter out from behind the PC and raise it off the floor, and you'll notice a marked increase in signal strength. The same thing goes with your wireless router; if it's hidden behind other equipment, you'll reduce its transmission range.

Along the same lines, you may be able to improve performance by moving or redirecting the antenna on your router or wireless adapter. Radio signals are directional; swiveling the antenna one direction or another can make a world of difference.

Move Devices That Might Cause Interference

Similarly, placing any wireless device (router or adapter) too close to other electronic equipment can reduce the effectiveness of the Wi-Fi signal. For example, I ran into problems when I placed my wireless router between a cordless phone and my computer monitor—both devices that generate their own electronic signals or fields. Simply moving the router to the other side of these devices dramatically increased its effective signal strength.

This last point reminds us that interference from other devices can affect the Wi-Fi signal. It's never a good idea to put your wireless router or adapter in close proximity to other cordless devices that use the 2.4GHz frequency band. In some instances, you may need to disconnect or turn off these other devices to get a clean Wi-Fi signal.

This type of interference can sometimes be minimized by changing the wireless broadcast channel used by your router and adapter. Every router has the option of transmitting on any one of multiple channels, which use different portions of the available 2.4GHz band. If multiple devices (or multiple networks—such as yours and a neighbor's) use the same channel, interference can result.

To change the channel that your equipment uses, run your wireless router's configuration utility. Consult your router's manual for specific instructions.

Finally, you can boost the range of your wireless signal by attaching an external antenna to your wireless router, or by using a wireless range extender device. Learn more about extending your signal in Chapter 16, "Upgrading Your Wireless Network."

Wireless Connection Is Intermittent

An intermittent wireless connection—one that keeps dropping and then reestablishing the wireless signal—can have many of the same causes as a weak signal. So if your connection keeps cutting in and out, make sure you work through all the items in the previous section.

Of course, intermittent connectivity can have other causes. Right click-the wireless connection icon, select Properties, then try the following:

- Disable 802.1X authentication (on the Security tab).
- Disable IPv6 functionality (on the Networking tab).
- Disable QoS Packet Scheduler (on the Networking tab).
- Uninstall the Link-Layer Topology Discovery Mapper I/O Driver and Responder (on the Networking tab).

You may need to reboot your computer after making any of these changes.

Finally, don't forget to check the device drivers for both the router and the wireless adapter. Updating to the latest versions can solve all sorts of oddball connection problems.

Can't Connect to the Internet

Here's a good one. You can make a clear connection to your wireless network, but then find you don't have access to the Internet. There can be several causes to this problem.

Verify That Your Internet Connection Is Up

First, make sure that your Internet connection is actually up and running. Make sure your broadband modem is turned on, that the cable connecting it to your cable or DSL line is properly connected, and that the Ethernet cable connecting it to your wireless modem is also properly connected.

Check the Status Lights on Your Modem

Next, look at the lights on the front of your modem. Do they indicate that the connection is up and running properly? If not, the problem is with your Internet service provider; call your ISP to report the issue. (And it might not hurt to power down your

Network TIP

To determine whether an Internet-related problem is with your modem or your router, connect your modem directly to your computer, bypassing the router. If everything works, you have a router-related issue. If the connection doesn't work, the problem is with your modem or Internet connection.

modem, wait 10 seconds or so, and then power it back up; rebooting a recalcitrant modem can fix all sorts of Internet connection problems.)

Rerun Your Router's Configuration Routine

It's also possible that your wireless router is not recognizing your Internet connection. Try rerunning the router's configuration routine to rediscover your particular connection.

Reboot Everything

Next, try an overall reboot of all the components in the system. In this order, reboot the modem, router, and computer, waiting for each to completely power back on before rebooting the next device.

Check IP Addressing

This problem can also be caused if your ISP provides a static IP address and your router is configured for a dynamic IP address. You may need to reconfigure your router for a static address, and then enter the information provided by your ISP: IP address for your router, address of the ISP's domain name server (DNS), and so forth. Consult your ISP for more details.

Run Network Diagnostics

The problem, of course, can also be with your computer. In particular, some sort of Winsock corruption can block access to an otherwise-good Internet connection. Fortunately, this is easily fixed by running Windows Vista's Network Diagnostics utility, as described earlier in this chapter.

Can't See Other Computers or Shared Folders on Your Network

You think you've made a good connection to your network. The signal strength looks good, and you have a solid Internet connection. But, for some reason, you can't see some or all of your network computers and folders when you open the Network Explorer. What to do?

Be Patient

First, have a little patience. When you first connect (or connect another computer) to the network, it can take up to 15 minutes for Windows and your router to find and display all your network computers. The same thing when you power up a computer that's been powered down or in hibernation; it takes a little time to wake up and recognize all the network neighbors.

Refresh Network Device List

Similarly, you may need to refresh the list of devices shown in the Network Explorer window. Right-click anywhere in the window and select Refresh from the pop-up window; then wait for all your network devices to be recognized.

Verify Power and Connections

If these methods don't do the trick, make sure that all your computers—your current one and the one(s) you can't see—are actually powered up and connected to the network. (Yes, that means opening the Start menu and selecting Connect To, just to make sure you're really connected.)

As to the power thing, you're sure *this* computer is powered up, but what about the one in the other room? It never hurts to check. Also, make sure the other computer isn't in sleep or hibernation mode; sleeping computers don't show up on the network.

While you're checking that other computer, see whether it can display your other network computer(s). If not, the problem is probably with that computer's network connection. Check all the cable connections, including the USB connection if it's using an external wireless adapter, and then reboot the computer.

Speaking of rebooting, if the problem persists on your first computer, reboot it. For whatever reason, "lost" computers on a network will often get found when you reboot the computer that can't see them.

Enable Network Discovery Feature

Another possibility is that Windows' network discovery feature is turned off. When network discovery is disabled, you can't see any other computers or devices on your network. To reenable network discovery, go the Network and Sharing Center, expand the Network Discovery option (in the Sharing and Discovery section), select On, and then click Apply.

By the way, if network discovery is disabled on the other computer, it won't be able to be seen by other computers on your network. Make sure you check the network discovery setting on the "invisible" computer, as well.

Check the Workgroup

Here's something else to check. If you've connected a Windows Vista computer to a Windows XP network, or vice versa, it's possible that your XP computers might be on a different workgroup than your Vista computers. You'll want to check the workgroup name for all the computers on your network and standardize any discrepancies.

To view the name of your workgroup on a Vista computer, open the Start menu, right-click Computer, and then click Properties; the workgroup name is displayed in the resulting System window. To change the workgroup name, click Change Settings to display the System Properties dialog box; then select the Computer Name tab and click the Change button. When the Computer Name/Domain Changes dialog box appears, enter a new name into the Workgroup field, click OK, and then proceed to reboot your computer.

To view the workgroup name on a Windows XP computer, open the Start menu, right-click My Computer, and then click Properties; when the System Properties dialog box appears, select the Computer Name tab to view the workgroup name. To change the workgroup name, click the Change button.

Check Your Software Firewall

Also, don't forget the old firewall bugaboo. An improperly configured or overly aggressive firewall can block all sorts of access to and from other computers on your network. First try turning off the firewall (on both computers) and then reconfigure it if you determine that's where the problem lies.

Verify That File Sharing Is Enabled

Finally, if you can see a computer but can't see or access its shared folders, it's possible that file sharing hasn't been enabled on that computer. It's also possible that file sharing is enabled but that you haven't been assigned access for that particular folder. Check the configuration of the other computer to make sure that proper access has been set.

Can't See Windows XP Computers on the Windows Vista Network Map

This is a common problem; actually, XP computers don't show up on the network map by default. That's because the map displays only those computers that have Link-Layer Topology Discovery (LLTD) installed, and most XP installations don't include LLTD.

If you have a Windows XP computer that doesn't appear on the network map, you can make it show up by installing LLTD on that machine. See the download and installation instructions at support.microsoft.com/kb/922120. After LLTD is installed on the XP machine, it should appear in its proper place on your Vista network map.

Can't Connect to Your Corporate Network from Home

Windows' VPN functionality can be a bit buggy at times—and it's not always the fault of Windows. That's because VPN depends on the configuration of the host corporate network as much as it depends on your computer's configuration.

When you can't connect to your corporate network via VPN, here are some things to try:

- Make sure that your corporate network has VPN enabled.
- Make sure you you've entered the correct VPN server name, as well as the correct network username and password.
- Check with your network administrator to make sure you have the correct permissions to remotely access the corporate network.
- If you're using special company software to connect, there could be a configuration or compatibility problem with this software. Contact your network administrator for assistance.
- Disable the firewall on your computer, which can sometimes block this sort of VPN connection.
- Make sure your computer is configured to use IPv4, not IPv6.

When all else fails, contact your network administrator or corporate technical support staff. It's to your company's benefit for you to use the network when you're out of the office; it's the company's job to help you get connected.

Lost or Can't Remember Your Router Password

Let's be honest. Reconfiguring your router is not something you do every day. If you set up your network in January and then find you need to reconfigure something in August, it's not unthinkable that you can't remember the password you need to enter to use the router's configuration utility.

Of course, it's possible that you didn't reset the router's default username or password. Try entering **admin** for the username and either **password** or **1234** as the password. (These are the most common defaults—and it's a good idea to change those defaults so that others can't do what you're trying to do now.)

If this doesn't work, most routers have some sort of reset button somewhere on the device, typically on the back or bottom of the unit. Press and hold down this reset button for 15 seconds or so, and the router will be reset to its default factory settings—and its default username and password.

> **Network CAUTION**
>
> Resetting a router to its factory default settings will reset *every* configuration change you've made to the router. In short, after you do the reset, you'll probably have to rerun the entire configuration routine—in essence, reinstalling your router from scratch.

Lost or Can't Remember Your WEP or WPA Passphrase

A similar problem exists if you can't remember your wireless security network key or passphrase. And if you can't remember the passphrase, you can't connect other computers to your network.

The solution here is much simpler. All you have to do is rerun the security configuration on your router and when doing so establish a new network key or passphrase. Make sure you write down this new passphrase, and then use it to configure wireless security on all your other network computers.

Can't Access Your Router's Configuration Utility

Can't remember how to access your wireless router's configuration utility? Well, if the utility doesn't show up anywhere on the Windows Start menu, try opening your web browser and entering **192.168.0.1** as the URL. This is the IP address used by most consumer wireless routers and should open the router's configuration utility in your web browser.

Of course, this won't work if the computer you're using isn't physically connected (via Ethernet) to the router. For security's sake, most routers do not allow configuration via a wireless connection. So dig out that Ethernet cable, connect it between your PC and the router, and *then* do the configuration thing.

Next: Start Using Your Network!

And with that, you're done reading this book—at least for the first time. There's a lot of useful reference information between these two covers, so don't throw the book away; keep it for future use, in case you have to connect a new device or troubleshoot some sort of network problem. Let's hope that your network is properly set up and configured, and that you can confidently share files, media, and devices between all your network PCs. That's the way it's supposed to work, after all.

Glossary

10/100   Networking components that support both 10Mbps (10BaseT) and 100Mbps (Fast Ethernet) technologies.

10Base-T   A networking standard for operating Ethernet networks at a 10Mbps transmission rate.

100Base-T   A networking standard for operating Ethernet networks at a 100Mbps transmission rate. Also known as Fast Ethernet.

192.168.0.1   The default IP address for many network routers. This address is set by the manufacturer at the factory but can be manually changed by the user at any time. When you enter this IP address into your web browser, you access the router's configuration utility.

2.4GHz   That portion of the RF band (actually located between 2.4 and 2.4835GHz) used by 802.11b/g/n Wi-Fi networks.

5GHz   That portion of the RF band (actually located between 5.725 and 5.850GHz) used by 802.11a Wi-Fi networks.

802.11a   One of several Wi-Fi specifications, operating at 54Mbps in the 5GHz RF band.

802.11b   One of several Wi-Fi specifications, operating at 11Mbps in the 2.4GHz RF band.

802.11g   One of several Wi-Fi specifications, operating at 54Mbps in the 2.4GHz RF band.

802.11n   An as-yet unfinalized Wi-Fi specification, operating at up to 540Mbps in the 2.4GHz RF band. So-called "Draft 2.0" equipment has been certified in advance of the final specification.

802.16   See *WiMAX*.

access point   A network device that transmits and receives wireless data.

adapter   A device that connects a computer to a wired or wireless network. A wireless adapter adds wireless transmission and reception to its host computer.

address   The unique location of any device on a network or the Internet.

AES   Advanced Encryption System. A 128-bit encryption scheme used in WPA2 wireless security.

bandwidth   On a computer network, the data transfer rate, typically measured in bits per second (bps).

bps   Bits per second. A measurement of data transfer speeds. As the name implies, this measures the number of data bits transmitted or received each second.

bridge   A device that connects two different types of networks. For example, an Ethernet bridge connects an Ethernet network or device to a wireless network.

broadband   Any type of Internet connection that is faster than traditional dial-up connections. Broadband connections are generally thought to be no slower than 256Kbps. Both digital cable and DSL are broadband connections.

DHCP   Dynamic Host Configuration Protocol. A networking protocol that lets one device on a local network assign temporary IP addresses to the other network devices.

DNS   Domain Name System (or Server or Service). An Internet service that translates domain names into IP addresses.

domain name   A text-based web address that defines one or more IP addresses. Domain names are used in URLs to identify web pages and websites.

DoS   Denial of Service. A type of computer attack where multiple communications are sent to a single server or domain in an attempt to overwhelm the underlying system.

DSL   Digital Subscriber Line. A type of broadband Internet connection that utilizes spare bandwidth in traditional phone lines.

dynamic IP address   A temporary IP address assigned by a DHCP server.

EAP   Extensible Authentication Protocol. A user authentication scheme used in WPA wireless security.

encryption   The translation of data into a secret code as a means to achieve data security. Most encryption methods use some sort of password or key to encode and decode the data.

Ethernet   A networking architecture (developed by Xerox in the mid-1970s) that enables the transfer of data over local area networks. Ethernet is a wired technology, utilizing self-named Ethernet cables. There are several variations of the basic Ethernet standard, all operating at different transfer speeds: 10Base-T (10Mbps), Fast Ethernet (100Mbps), and Gigabit Ethernet (1Gbps).

Extreme G   A variation on the 802.11g Wi-Fi standard that effectively doubles the transmission speeds to 108Mbps.

Fast Ethernet   A networking standard for operating Ethernet networks at a 100Mbps transmission rate. Also known as 100Base-T.

firewall   A software program or piece of hardware that functions as a barrier to access from outside a network or individual computer.

gateway   (1) A node or device on a network that functions as an entrance to another network. (2) A device that combines a wireless router with a broadband modem, typically provided by cable or DSL ISPs.

Gbps Gigabits per second; one million bits per second. A measurement of data transmission speed.

GHz Gigahertz. One million cycles per second. A measurement of frequency.

gigabit One million bits. A measurement of data size.

Gigabit Ethernet A networking standard for operating Ethernet networks at a 1Gbps (1,000Mbps) transmission rate.

hot spot A public Wi-Fi network that provides wireless access to the Internet, typically via use of an access point or wireless router.

HTTP Hypertext Transfer Protocol. The underlying protocol for the World Wide Web that defines how data is formatted and transmitted.

hub A simple network switch that transmits data from a single input port to multiple output ports. With a hub, every computer connected to the hub receives all data sent by any other computer. Similar to a switch or router, but with much less routing intelligence.

ICS Internet Connection Sharing. A Windows-based technology that enables the sharing of a single Internet connection, connected to a gateway computer, with other computers on a network.

IP Internet Protocol. The protocol used to send data over a network; IP specifies the format of data packets and the addressing scheme.

IP address The address used to identify a computer or device on a network.

IPsec IP security. A set of protocols designed to support secure exchange of data packets over a network, at the IP layer. Typically used in Virtual Private Networks (VPNs).

IPv4 Internet Protocol version 4. An older version of the Internet Protocol, still widely used today. Utilizes a 32-bit addressing scheme, in the form of 123.4.56.789.

IPv6 Internet Protocol version 6. The newest version of the Internet Protocol, successor to IPv4. Utilizes a 128-bit addressing scheme, in the form of 1234:1db4:1:1:1:12ab. This provides a much larger universe of potential addresses than with IPv4.

ISP Internet Service Provider. A company that provides access to the Internet, typically for a monthly fee.

Kbps Kilobits per second; 1,000 bits per second. A measurement of data transmission speed.

KHz Kilohertz; 1,000 cycles per second. A measurement of frequency.

LAN Local Area Network. A computer network that spans a relatively small area, typically a single location.

LLTD Link Layer Topology Discovery. A Windows-based protocol, developed by Microsoft, for the discovery of the physical configuration of a network.

MAC address   Media Access Control address. The unique hardware address of a device connected to a network.

malware   Malicious software. Any computer program designed specifically to damage or disrupt a system. Both spyware and viruses are malware.

Mbps   Megabits per second; one million bits per second. A measurement of data transmission speed.

MHz   Megahertz. One million cycles per second. A measurement of frequency or speed.

MIMO   Multiple-In Multiple-Out. A type of multiplexing that utilizes multiple antennas to increase bandwidth and range over a wireless network. MIMO is a feature of the 802.11n Wi-Fi protocol.

modem   Modulator-demodulator. A device that converts digital data to analog form for transmission over analog lines. Typically used to connect a computer to the Internet, via either phone or cable lines.

NAS   Network Attached Storage. A hard disk or server that connects to a network, typically directly to a network router, and provides data storage for all computers connected to the network.

network   Two or more computers or similar devices connected together, typically for the purpose of sharing data, peripherals, or an Internet connection.

network key   An encrypted password or passphrase used to access a network protected with wireless security.

network name   See *SSID*.

NIC   Network Interface Card. A board that inserts inside a personal computer to provide Ethernet capability.

packet   A unit of data transmitted over a network.

passphrase   The password used in various wireless security schemes. A passphrase is typically longer and more complex than a simple password, often incorporating a long string of numbers, letters, and special characters.

ping   A utility used to determine whether a particular IP address on a network or the Internet is accessible. It works by sending a packet of data to the specified address, and then waits for a reply.

print server   A device that enables a printer to be connected directly to a network, without first connecting to a host computer. Print servers can be either wired or wireless.

protocol   An agreed upon format for transmitting data between two or more devices.

repeater   See *wireless extender*.

RF Radio frequency. Any frequency within the electromagnetic spectrum that allows the transmission of radio waves. Most wireless networking technologies utilize some segment of the RF spectrum.

router A device that forwards data packets between devices on a network. In this regard, a router (also known as a hub) is similar to a network switch, but with the added capability of connecting to another network or the Internet. Routers can be either wired or wireless; most wireless routers also incorporate a wireless access point.

server Any computer on a network used to provide user access to files, printing, and other services.

spyware A piece of software that surreptitiously installs itself on a computer and then sends user information to another computer, typically over the Internet.

SSID Service Set Identifier. A unique 32-bit name used to identify a given wireless network. Also known as a *network name*.

subnet A portion of a network that shares a common address component. On a TCP/IP network, a subnet consists of all devices whose IP addresses have the same numeric prefix.

subnet mask A means of determining which subnet a specific IP address belongs to.

switch A device that channels incoming data on a network from an input port to a specific output port. Offers more routing intelligence than a simple network hub, but less than that of a network router.

TCP Transmission Control Protocol. A networking protocol that enables two devices to establish a connection and exchange streams of data.

TCP/IP Transmission Control Protocol/Internet Protocol. The suite of communications protocols used to connect devices over a network or the Internet.

TKIP Temporal Key Integrity Protocol. A data encryption scheme used in WPA wireless security. TKIP scrambles the network key, using a particular algorithm.

UAC User Account Control. A new security feature in Windows Vista that restricts the use of Administrator accounts and privileges.

UPnP Universal Plug and Play. A networking architecture that provides compatibility among equipment and software offered by participating manufacturers.

URL Uniform Resource Locator. The address of a web page or other document on the World wide Web. The URL contains the protocol of the resource (http:// for web pages, ftp:// for FTP sites, and so forth), the domain name or IP address of the website, and the specific name of the file or page.

virus A software program or piece of program code that is loaded onto a computer without the user's knowledge, typically designed to somehow harm or disrupt the host system. Computer viruses are capable of replicating themselves and can thus be passed from computer to computer.

VoIP   Voice over IP (Internet Protocol). A category of hardware and software that enables people to use the Internet as a transmission medium for voice telephone calls.

VPN   Virtual Private Network. A private data network that can be accessed via the Internet or traditional phone lines, while providing privacy via various security procedures.

WAN   Wide Area Network. A computer network that spans a wide geographic area, typically multiple physical locations. Most WANs consist of two or more LANS.

WCN   Windows Connect Now. New technology in Windows Vista that lets you save the network settings from your main computer to a USB flash drive, for easier setup of other computers on your network.

WEP   Wired Equivalent Privacy. An older, less robust security protocol for wireless networks, designed to provide the same level of security as a wired network. The weakest level of WEP security provides 64-bit encryption; the strongest level provides 128-bit encryption.

Wi-Fi   Wireless Fidelity. Any wireless technology incorporating some version of the 802.11 wireless standard.

WiMAX   Technology utilizing the 802.16 specification for fixed broadband metropolitan networks—broadband citywide wireless Internet.

wireless adapter   A network adapter that adds wireless transmission/reception to a computer or similar device.

wireless extender   A device that extends the range of an existing wireless network, by effectively repeating or rebroadcasting the network signal.

wireless security   Any scheme that limits public access to a wireless network, typically via the use of encrypted network keys or passphrases.

WLAN   Wireless LAN (Local Area Network).

workgroup   Two or more computers connected to the same network. Workgroups are typically named separately from the wireless network name.

WPA   Wi-Fi Protected Access. A wireless security scheme used in Wi-Fi networking. More secure than the older WEP security, but superseded by the newer WPA2 standard.

WPA2   The newest version of WPA security, enhanced via network keys that are changed on a regular basis.

WPA-PSK   WPA Pre-Shared Key. The component of WPA wireless security that requires the use of an encrypted passphrase to access the network.

Index

X–Z

THIS BOOK IS SAFARI ENABLED

INCLUDES FREE 45-DAY ACCESS TO THE ONLINE EDITION

The Safari® Enabled icon on the cover of your favorite technology book means the book is available through Safari Bookshelf. When you buy this book, you get free access to the online edition for 45 days.

Safari Bookshelf is an electronic reference library that lets you easily search thousands of technical books, find code samples, download chapters, and access technical information whenever and wherever you need it.

TO GAIN 45-DAY SAFARI ENABLED ACCESS TO THIS BOOK:

- Go to **http://www.quepublishing.com/safarienabled**
- Complete the brief registration form
- Enter the coupon code found in the front of this book on the "Copyright" page

If you have difficulty registering on Safari Bookshelf or accessing the online edition, please e-mail customer-service@safaribooksonline.com.